Best Bike Rides®

D0205620

THE BEST BIKE RIDES® IN NEW YORK, NEW JERSEY, AND PENNSYLVANIA

by

Trudy E. Bell
revised by Dale Lally

The Globe Pequot Press

Guilford, Connecticut

Cover design: Saralyn D'Amato-Twomey
Cover photograph: Courtesy of Pearl Izumi/John Kelly
Map design: Erin E. Hernandez
Interior photos: p. viii, p. 9: Dale Lally; p. 109, p. 229: Trudy Bell; p. 147: Mark Scholefield

Library of Congress Cataloging-in-Publication Data
Bell, Trudy E.
    Best bike rides in New York, New Jersey, and Pennsylvania /by Trudy E. Bell and Dale Lally. — 1st ed.
            p.   cm.—(Best bike rides series)
        ISBN 0-7627-0475-6
    1. Bicycle touring—New York (State) Guidebooks. 2. Bicycle touring—New Jersey guidebooks. 3. Bicycle touring—Pennsylvania Guidebooks. 4. New York (State) guidebooks. 5. New Jersey Guidebooks. 6. Pennsylvania Guidebooks. I. Lally, Dale. II. Title. III. Series.
    GV1045.5.N72B45 1999
    917.404'43—dc21   99-31194
                                                                            CIP

Manufactured in the United States of America
First Edition/First Printing

THE BEST
BIKE RIDES®
IN NEW YORK,
NEW JERSEY,
AND
PENNSYLVANIA

Help Us Keep This Guide Up to Date

Every effort has been made by the author and editors to make this guide as accurate and useful as possible. However, many things can change after a guide is published—establishments close, phone numbers change, facilities come under new management, and so on.

We would love to hear from you concerning your experiences with this guide and how you feel it could be improved and be kept up to date. While we may not be able to respond to all comments and suggestions, we'll take them to heart and we'll also make certain to share them with the author. Please send your comments and suggestions to the following address:

The Globe Pequot Press
Reader Response/Editorial Department
P.O. Box 480
Guilford, CT 06437

Or you may e-mail us at:

editorial@globe-pequot.com

Thanks for your input, and happy travels!

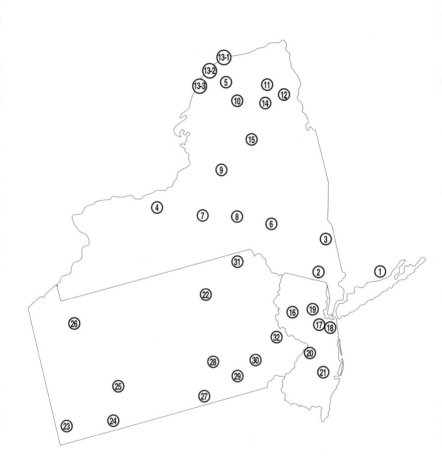

Contents

Introduction

Bike Rides

Appendix

Introduction

The Best Bike Rides in New York, New Jersey, and Pennsylvania

New York, New Jersey, and Pennsylvania offer fantasically beautiful world-class areas for bicycle touring—easily the equal to any region in the United States.

Because these states were settled centuries ago, when many byways were still footpaths and dirt wagon tracks joined local communities, the area offers a vast network of wandering secondary and tertiary roads bypassed by the more direct interstate and toll highways. Even in today's automobile-oriented society, these small roads are almost undisturbed by cars—and they pass through some of the loveliest countryside a cyclist could hope for.

For scenery you can choose fragrant pine forests, cultivated farm fields, or meandering river valleys. For terrain you have the choice of virtually flat (on New York's Long Island and in southern New Jersey), rolling (in southeastern Pennsylvania), or hilly (upstate New York). Stop to pet the horses standing next to the rails of a horse farm; pick your own apples in the fall at wayside orchards; open your picnic lunch next to a waterfall; pedal through great Civil War battlefields. And after the day's exercise, camp under the stars in the bracing forest air or luxuriate in a soaking bath at a bed-and-breakfast inn. These and other choices are offered on this book's lovely routes, which were contributed by local bicycle clubs, state tourism organizations, commercial bicycle touring groups, and dedicated individual cyclists.

Some of the rides take you through areas that are the acknowledged favorite of many cyclists—such as the Pennsylvania Dutch farm land and the Finger Lakes region of New York.

On a summer weekend in those areas, you are very likely to exchange a wave and a smile with dozens of other riders you pass on the road. Other routes guide you through places as yet largely undiscovered by road-touring cyclists, such as the tour of the St. Lawrence Valley or the South Colton tour. Thus, you can even choose a ride based on the society or solitude you seek!

Something for Everyone

To aid in your selection, the rides in this book are categorized by their difficulty.

Rambles are the easiest, designed to be completed by almost anyone; they are under 35 miles long, and their terrain is flat or gently rolling.

Cruises are intermediate in difficulty, ranging from 25 to 50 miles, with the terrain being rolling or moderately hilly.

Challenges require adequate training and preparation; they range from 40 to 70 miles in total distance and may include long climbs.

Classics, the equivalent of the "black diamond" slopes in skiing, are longer than 60 miles, and their terrain may be hilly or mountainous; they will satisfy the strong, expert rider.

Having noted this, less experienced riders should *not* be discouraged from trying one of the challenges or classics in this guide. Although the rides are named after their longest incarnation, there are often cutoffs to turn them into shorter cruises or rambles. Alternatively, some of the longer rides can be broken up into shorter segments by staying overnight along the way. This is particularly true with the Adirondack Gran Tour and the Tour of the St. Lawrence Valley.

As terrain is as much a factor as distance in determining a ride's difficulty, please note that some long rides that are very flat (such as the 51-mile-long "Strawberries and Wine Cruise" on Long Island) may be easier than some short rides (such as the 32-mile-long Endless Mountains Challenge in Pennsylvania, which has a genuine killer hill).

How to Use This Book

Each ride is preceded by a short description to give you a feel for the specific area and what you are likely to see. The description usually mentions roadside attractions, as well as inns or campgrounds for spending the night; where possible, telephone numbers are also provided.

The most crucial section of the description is "The Basics." There you will find information about the ride's mileage, including mileage options for shortened routes; terrain; automobile traffic; and availability of food. Where possible, the routes start near public rest rooms, water, and sources of food, but for a few of the more isolated rides, you will have to bring all your provisions with you.

Last is "Miles & Directions"—a cue sheet, in bicycle-touring parlance. For the uninitiated, a cue sheet contains the actual directions for cycling. The normal cue sheet will include a starting point plus detailed instructions as to the direction of travel, segment length, and where to turn. It will very often include information on landmarks. While there are variations, with some cue sheets offering extensive background materials, the normal cue sheet will provide this basic information. Also, as much as possible, this book observes several conventions. A "T intersection" is one where the road you are on dead-ends into a perpendicular road where you must turn either left or right. A "Y intersection" is one where the road you are on appears to split into a fork.

A word about maps: Take several. The best is a county map showing all the local streets. (*Note:* Some rides pass through several counties. The names of the counties are given for every ride.) Ideally, if you can find more than one map put out by different publishers, take along two or more. Why weigh yourself down that way? First, maps can help you spontaneously shortcut or add to your ride midway through it, beyond what's shown in this book. Second, road construction begun after this book's publication may block off part of the directed route, in which case a supplemental map can help you find a detour and guide you back to the main route. (If this happens to you, please write to the authors so that the rides can be correctly updated in subsequent editions; see "A Modest Request" and "Disclaimer" on pages 7 and 8. Third, as maps do contain errors in the way roads are drawn and labeled, having two maps by different publishers allows you to compare the versions to ascertain which one better matches your current situation. For more information see "State Bicycling Maps and Guides" in the Appendix.

Safety and Comfort on the Road

Like skiing, boating, and many other sports, bicycling has distinct hazards, some of which have claimed lives. But the chance of injury can be minimized by proper equipment and technique. Moreover, there are ways to increase your comfort, allowing you to enjoy hours in the saddle day after day.

Most important of all: Always wear a helmet. If you bicycle regularly, it is not a matter of *if* you will fall but of *when*. A helmet can make the difference between a serious injury that ends your journey or just some road rash and a story to tell. For maximum protection buy one that has the sticker inside indicating that it has passed the rigorous safety standards of the Snell Memorial Foundation. A white or yellow helmet will reflect the sun's heat the best and offer maximum visibility at night. Adjust the inside fit of the helmet with the different sized pads provided. You want the helmet to hold on to your head firmly enough to stay on when you bend over upside down even without the chin strap fastened. Then adjust the chin strap so it's loose enough to be comfortable when your neck is extended forward but taut enough so the helmet cannot be pushed backward off your forehead.

Wear fingerless, padded cycling gloves for two reasons: to buffer road shock to your hands as you ride and to minimize abrasion should you fall. Even roads that look smooth are bumpy enough to make unprotected palms and heels of your hands feel weary at the end of a day's ride. Plus, the open oval on the back above the glove's closure will give the backs of your hands the characteristic "bicyclist's suntan," which can be a nice conversation-starter in social situations!

Use a rear-view mirror to monitor automobile traffic approaching from behind. With a mirror you will not be startled if a car suddenly materializes to your left and honks. Also, you will not have to take your eyes off the road ahead to know what is going on behind. The most effective rear-view mirrors mount to your helmet or eyeglasses; the ones that mount to your bicycle handlebars may vibrate too much to stay aligned or to produce a clear image.

Wear light, bright colors so you are visible to motorists, particularly on overcast days or toward sunset. Yellow is the best of both worlds. Some neon colors, such as neon yellow and lime, are even better. For maximum visibility apply reflective tape to your bicycle frame and helmet, especially if there's a chance you'll be riding after dark. Headlights and taillights for the bicycle, required by many states, also alert motorists to your presence.

Last, **ride defensively.** The traffic laws in most states recognize the bicycle as a vehicle, with all the rights and responsibilities thereof. That means stopping at all stop signs and red lights, using left-turn lanes, and using arm signals to indicate your intentions. On roads where you must share the right-hand lane with vehicular traffic, rely on your ears and your rear-view mirror to monitor cars and trucks approaching you from behind. Do not block your ears with earphones; not only are they illegal, but they will deprive you of auditory warnings. Most state laws call for cyclists to ride as far to the right as practicable—but "as far right as practicable" does not necessarily mean blindly clinging to the far right-hand edge in all circumstances. On fast downhills where you feel insecure at the far right because the road's edge is broken or littered with gravel, you are legally permitted to take the lane—that is, to ride far enough to the left (about where the passenger in a car would sit) so that cars approaching from behind must slow down to pass you—and then immediately move back again to the right when the hazard is passed or you're traveling slower again. When passing parked cars, look carefully inside each for the silhouettes of heads of people who might suddenly open a door in your path. Buy a cyclist's bell, the loudest one you can find, and use it to warn cars and pedestrians of your presence; do *not* use a police whistle—not only is it illegal in some places, but it often offends people, and many times they do not think the whistle blast applies to them. For more information on safe techniques for riding in traffic, read John Forester's classic *Effective Cycling,* 6th edition (MIT Press, 1992).

Now that you're equipped for safety, here are a few additional words about simple comfort.

Padded cycling shorts will minimize saddle-soreness. Saddle-soreness is produced by the transmission of road shock from your saddle through soft flesh to your "sit bones" (ischial tuberosity). The most effective padding is made of genuine or artificial chamois; polypropylene is more effective for wicking away moisture than protecting against saddle-soreness. For additional protection you can buy a seat cover of either sheepskin or gel; both are equally effective, although the gel has a longer lifetime. A bonus: Cycling shorts, which usually extend down to the knee, also protect the skin of your inner thighs against chafing and blisters that otherwise can be caused by rubbing against either the saddle itself or the seam of ordinary short or long pants.

Bicycling jerseys also serve several practical purposes. Their light colors increase your visibility; their polypropylene or wool fabric increases the wicking of perspiration to keep you dry; their longer cut in the rear shields your lower back from the sun and wind; and their rear pockets allow you to carry a wallet and keys without your legs hitting them at the top of every pedal stroke.

Take at least one water bottle, and always pack a minimum "emergency snack" of raisins or Fig Newtons, even for the shortest rides. On hot days pack a salty snack as well; ideal are pretzels, which are also low in fat and high in complex carbohydrates.

A word about tools: As many of these routes deliberately take you away from human habitation, you may not find a bike shop nearby. Take bicycle tools—at the very least, tire levers, a patch kit, and a pump for repairing a flat tire—and either know how to use them or travel with a friend who does. In fact, if you anticipate bicycling a lot, one of the best favors you can do yourself is to sign up for a simple "roadside bicycle repair" class, offered by many continuing education schools, bicycle clubs, and youth hostels. If you lack knowledge and tools, a simple flat tire can immobilize you for hours, requiring you to flag down a van or truck to take you back to civilization, whereas if you're equipped, you can fix the problem and be back on the road again in less than twenty minutes.

A Modest Request

If readers pedaling these routes have suggested corrections, updates, or additions, we would be grateful to receive them for a subsequent edition. Moreover, we would welcome the contribution of altogether different rides to round out the geographic representation of the best bike rides in the region. Also, if you would enjoy being a volunteer to verify rides for a later edition, we'd love to hear from you. Please send changes for the existing rides, cue sheets and maps for new rides, or any other comments to us c/o The Globe Pequot Press, P.O. Box 480, Guilford, CT 06437.

New York

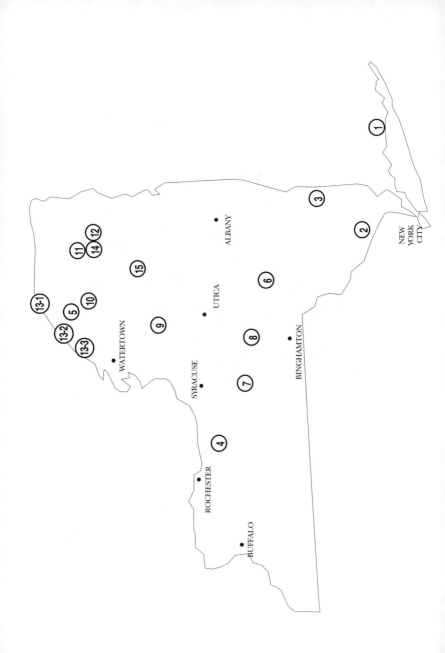

New York

Strawberries and Wine Cruise

Mattituck—Greenport—Orient Point—Mattituck

This flat ride is based in part on the traditional annual "Strawberry Ride" of New York City's American Youth Hostels and was verified by Gil Gilmore of Norwalk, Connecticut. It starts at the town of Mattituck on the north fork of Long Island, which holds a strawberry festival each June in the fields of Mattituck High School. (For the date of the festival and also a possible change in venue, call the Greenport-Southold Chamber of Commerce at 516–477–1383.)

If after all that strawberry shortcake you can manage to swing your leg over your bicycle saddle, the route will take you through some of Suffolk County's best wine country. You'll pedal right past half a dozen vineyards, many of which offer public tours and wine tasting—Peconic Bay Vineyards, Pugliese Vineyards, Bedell Cellars, Pindar Winery, and Lenz Winery—and you can visit more by looking for signs with a symbol of grapes directing you down local side roads. Just use good judgment in sampling the wares: It's even more dangerous to bicycle than to drive under the influence of alcohol, as you are not surrounded by a ton of protective steel.

The midpoint of the ride—perfect for lunch—is a favorite destination for cyclists: Orient Beach State Park, with its refreshment stand, seafood cafe, bathhouse, and pebbly beach overlooking the sparkling Atlantic. This is also the trailhead for a 2-mile hike out to the bird sanctuary at the very tip of Long Beach Point. The park is friendly to cyclists, complete with bike lane on the highway (although it compels you to ride at least part of both directions facing traffic), and is open every day of the year excepting Tuesday.

Elsewhere on the ride you'll pass some churches and houses dating from the American Revolution, plus an old lighthouse commissioned by George Washington and now turned into a marine museum. Amateur astronomers might try to time their visit for one of the Saturday observing nights at the Custer Institute Observatory in Southold (516–765–2626), the only astronomical observatory on Long Island that lets the public look through its telescopes.

Those wishing to make a long weekend of the visit can stay in one of the lovely bed-and-breakfast inns on Shelter Island (for a listing call the Shelter Island Chamber of Commerce at 516–749–0399), a detour that's just a five-minute ferry ride from Greenport. Shelter Island's rolling hills, beaches, and lightly traveled roads offer superb cycling—a nice change of pace from the flat terrain of the basic tour on Long Island's north fork.

Although you'll be pedaling on some main roads on this ride (because some parts of the north fork are so narrow that there is only one road), Long Island is civilized in offering wide paved shoulders. Just be careful: In some places the shoulder is an inch below the pavement of the main road, and brushing that lip with your tire could cause a spill.

A word about Long Island weather: The eastern tip of Long Island is the last place in the New York City tri-state area that the seasons linger. Thus, the chill of winter lasts into mid-April, but summer's warmth lingers past September. After Labor Day is perhaps the best time for cycling: You miss the frenetic summer crowds but can swim in the ocean while it's still bathwater-warm.

The Basics

Start: Mattituck, in the parking lot of the Long Island Rail Road station. Take the Long Island Expressway to its end at exit 73 and then take Rte. 25 farther east to Mattituck. In town turn left at the traffic light onto Love Ln. and then left into the parking lot of the train station.

Length: 51 miles.

Terrain: Virtually flat, although you are likely to run into substantial headwinds while traveling eastward. Traffic ranges from light on the side roads to moderate on the main roads.

Food: Widely available in the various towns and at the concession and restaurants at Orient Beach State Park. But best of all are farm stands: Take advantage of the fresh local produce!

Miles & Directions

- 0.0 Turn left out of the parking lot of the Mattituck station of the Long Island Rail Road, making an immediate right onto Love Ln.
- 0.1 If you're going to the strawberry festival, turn left at the T intersection onto Rte. 25E (Main Rd.) until you reach Mattituck High School; otherwise turn right onto Rte. 25W.
- 0.2 Turn left at the Handy Pantry convenience store onto New Suffolk Ave.
- 3.2 Turn left at the four-way flashing stop light onto 5th St., which becomes New Suffolk Rd. At this intersection, Olsson's Deli is very bicycle-friendly with decent food and rest rooms.
- 5.0 Turn right at the light onto Rte. 25E (Main Rd.). You'll now stay on Rte. 25E through all its incarnations for the next 15 miles. In the next 3 miles, you'll pass half a dozen wineries. At mile 9.3 you can turn right onto Corwin Ln. and make an immediate right onto Bayview Rd. to visit the Custer Institute Observatory. At mile 13.3 you'll

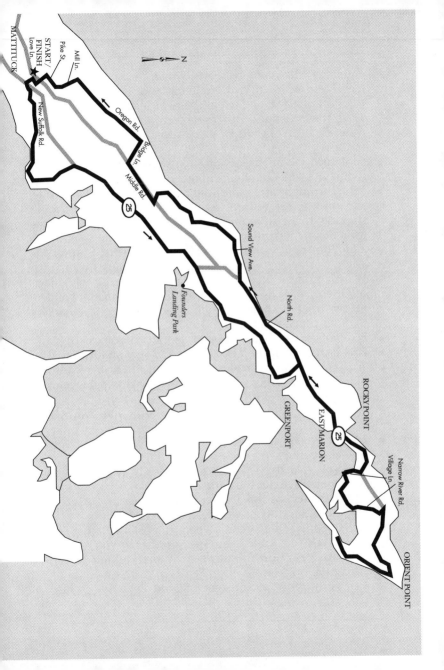

enter the village of Greenport, where the traffic gets heavier. If you want to visit Shelter Island, at mile 14.1 turn right onto 5th St. and left at the next block (Wiggins St.) to reach the ferry dock. Otherwise continue to follow Rte. 25E (now called Front St.) straight into Greenport. Watch for traffic!

- 14.4 Turn left at the flashing red signal (T intersection) to follow Rte. 25E out of Greenport.
- 15.4 Turn right at the flashing red signal (T intersection) to stay on Rte. 25E toward Orient Point. There is a nice wide shoulder to use from here to Orient Point; this is the beginning of a signed official bike route.
- 19.6 Turn right onto Village Ln., marked with a grassy triangle containing a small obelisk resembling a miniature Washington Monument. You are now entering the village of Orient, with its sparkling bay views and many wonderful centuries-old homes. Stop to read the historical markers to steep yourself in the mood.
- 20.1 Follow the road as it bends left and becomes King St.
- 20.4 Bear right at the Y intersection to stay on King St.
- 20.7 Turn left at the end (yield sign) onto Narrow River Rd. This is a truly lovely stretch past the swaying tall grasses of a salt marsh. Savor it through all its curves.
- 22.5 Turn right at the end (stop sign) onto Rte. 25E, which is now the only road out to Orient Point.
- 24.5 Turn right into Orient Beach State Park, taking the labeled bike route.
- 26.7 You've arrived! When you're ready to leave, retrace your route back out the park access road.
- 29.0 Turn left at the T intersection onto Rte. 25W, and keep pedaling straight west for the next 11 miles.
- 36.5 Keep heading straight where the yellow flasher marks Rte. 25W's turn back into Greenport; now you're on Rte. 48W. Use caution in riding on the shoulder, which is broken-up blacktop.
- 39.9 Turn right onto unsigned Sound View Ave., which is

bumpy but beautiful, with little traffic. This turn is the first right after the Soundview Restaurant.

- 41.1 Bear left at the fork to stay on Sound View Ave. (If you want a little historical detour, bear right instead; the road dead-ends at the Horton Point Lighthouse, now the home of the Southold Historical Society Marine Museum. It is open on weekend afternoons in July and August.) Go straight through two four-way stops. At mile 44.1 follow Sound View Ave. as it makes an abrupt left (Goldsmith's Inlet Park will be on your right) and becomes Mill Rd.
- 44.4 Turn right to rejoin Rte. 48W (here called Middle Rd.).
- 45.8 Turn right onto Bridge Ln.
- 46.5 Turn left at the end onto Oregon Rd., where you'll be cycling past farms and vineyards for the next 3 miles.
- 49.4 Turn left onto unsigned Mill Ln., an old concrete road. (Not many concrete roads are in this area.)
- 50.0 Turn right onto Wickham Ave., following it as it curves left through suburbs.
- 50.7 Turn left at the T intersection to stay on Wickham Ave.
- 51.1 After crossing Rte. 48 at the light, turn right onto Pike St. and follow it to Love Ln. and the Mattituck station of the Long Island Railroad.

2

New Croton Reservoir Ramble

Teatown Lake Reservation—Lincolndale—Yorktown Heights—Croton Dam—Teatown Lake Reservation

The area around the New Croton Reservoir, part of New York City's water supply, is a favorite of New York City cyclists because this wooded section of lower Westchester County is only 25 miles north of the city. Despite its proximity to what Frank Sinatra immortalized in song as "the city that never sleeps," Westchester County is characterized by wonderfully secluded backroads—in part because the county's affluent residents would rather have their restful homes passed by dirt tracks than paved thoroughfares. The result is a cyclist's dream.

One of the route's highlights is a ride across the top of the Croton Dam overlooking Croton Gorge Park below. Because most of the route hugs the shore of the reservoir, much of it is level to gently rolling, with lovely views of the sparkling water.

In fact, the inland terrain is so reminiscent of West Virginia or Vermont that Westchester County boasts one of the East Coast's two mountain-bike schools: Mike Zuckerman's Croton Mountain Biking Center (10 Sunset Trail, Croton-on-Hudson, NY 10520, 914–271–2640). This route leads you on a few of these peaceful roads, ruts and all, so you may find a fatter-tire bike more comfortable than a thin-tire racing bike.

Note: In this area, street signs seem to be battered, twisted, or missing altogether. Follow descriptions carefully.

Should you wish to make a weekend of your visit, you may well enjoy the luxury of a night at the rambling Alexander Hamilton House bed-and-breakfast inn, just a couple of miles from this route at 49 Van Wyck Street in Croton-on-Hudson (914–271–6737). The owner is Barbara Notarius, author of a book on running a bed-and-breakfast. Barbara suggested the basic route around the reservoir.

Teatown Lake Reservation, the start of this ride, is a wildlife preserve and environmental education center, with hiking trails as well as a small museum and gift shop.

The Basics

Start: Teatown Lake Reservation parking lot. To get there from the Taconic State Pkwy., exit at Route 134 toward Ossining; drive on Rte. 134W to the second right (which comes fast); turn right onto narrow Spring Valley Rd.; drive more than a mile to Teatown, going left at every fork. Turn right into the reservation parking lot.

Length: 20 or 24 miles.

Terrain: Gently rolling to moderately hilly. Traffic ranges from almost nonexistent on the true back roads to moderate on Rte. 129 around the north side of the New Croton Reservoir.

Food: Bring a full picnic lunch, as there are few services on any of these routes. Teatown Lake Reservation has a soda machine, and a couple of hotdog trucks have regular sites at dusty intersections as noted.

Miles & Directions

■ 0.0 Turn left out of the Teatown Lake Reservation Environ-

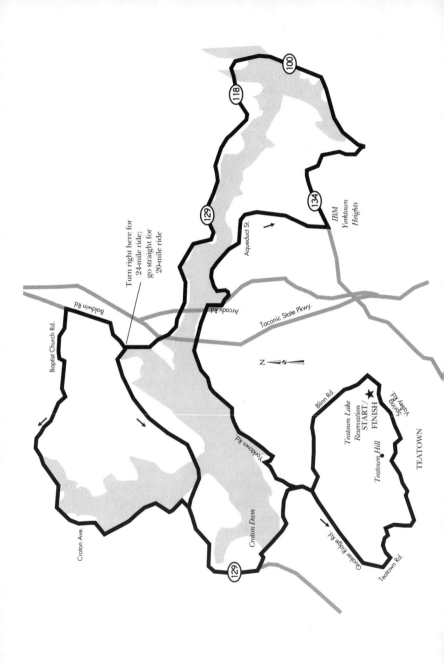

Turn right here for
24-mile ride;
go straight for
20-mile ride

100

118

129

134

IBM
Yorktown
Heights

Aqueduct St.

Baldwin Rd.

Arcady Rd.

Taconic State Pkwy.

N

Baptist Church Rd.

Yorktown Rd.

Blinn Rd.

Teatown Lake
Reservation
START /
FINISH

Spring
Valley Rd.

Croton Ave.

Croton Dam

129

Quaker Ridge Rd.

Teatown Hill

Teatown Rd.

TEATOWN

mental Education Center onto Spring Valley Rd.

- 0.1 Turn left onto narrow Blinn Rd., which becomes Applebee Farm Rd.
- 1.6 Turn right at the T intersection onto Quaker Ridge Rd. At mile 1.8 bear slightly right onto Yorktown Rd. where Croton Dam Rd. heads left. Shortly, the road will bend to the right and then to the left as it goes downhill. In about half a mile, the bumpy, broken pavement ends and the road becomes hard-packed dirt; go slowly, for there are many ruts. At miles 3.8 and 4.1, you'll pass under the Taconic State Pkwy.
- 4.3 Bear right at the Y intersection onto unmarked Arcady Rd., which begins climbing at mile 5.0 As you are climbing, and have the time to look, check out the old stone walls. Near the end, the road becomes Aqueduct St.
- 5.8 At the T intersection, just across from the entrance to IBM's Thomas J. Watson Research Center, turn left onto moderately busy Rte. 134.
- 7.5 After crossing a paved bicycle path, turn left at the T intersection onto moderately busy Rte. 100. At this intersection a hotdog truck is sometimes on your left. Ride with caution, for the next 1.3 miles has no shoulder. Have faith; it gets better. At mile 8.8 head straight at the first light to stay on the lane-wide painted shoulder of Rte. 100 over the bridge across the New Croton Reservoir.
- 9.3 Turn left at the traffic light onto Rte. 118; at this intersection another truck may be selling snacks.
- 11.1 At the flashing yellow light, keep heading straight onto Rte. 129 where Rte. 118 goes right.
- 13.3 Turn right onto Underhill Rd. (which is marked with a very large green sign) and begin climbing; you have now begun the rather challenging optional loop of rutted road and quiet beauty circling an inlet of the New Croton Reservoir.

For the 20-mile ride, do not turn right but instead continue straight on Rte. 129 and resume following the directions at mile 18.1.

- 13.7 Turn left onto Baldwin Rd. Watch carefully for this intersection, as it is easy to miss. Continue climbing, noting (if you can) the nice stone walls on both sides.
- 14.0 Turn left onto Baptist Church Rd. Now you're plunged into a very bumpy but gorgeous, forested roller-coaster ride. Be prepared also for a sharp downhill turn to the right halfway along.
- 15.7 At the stop sign make a quick jog left onto Hunter Brook Rd. (unmarked) and then immediately right to continue on unmarked Baptist Church Rd.
- 16.4 At the yield sign turn left onto Croton Ave., noting the island in the inlet on your left. This narrow section of road is level and smooth, with very few cars.
- 18.0 Turn right at the T intersection onto Short Hill Rd. Be careful here, as traffic from the left has a yield sign, not a stop sign. True to the road's name, you'll climb up a short, steep hill.
- 18.1 Bear right at the stop sign onto Rte. 129, rejoining the 20-mile route.
- 19.2 Turn left onto Croton Dam Rd. (shortly after the big intersection with Batten Rd.). Watch carefully for this almost hidden intersection after Rte. 129 starts descending. In a few moments you've climbed up to pedal across the top of the New Croton Dam. Very dramatic indeed.
- 20.1 Turn right at the T intersection onto unmarked Quaker Ridge Rd. (You'll recognize the intersection from the beginning of the ride, as Yorktown Rd. goes to the left.)
- 21.3 Turn left onto the beautiful Teatown Rd., taking note again of the stone walls. The last section of this one-lane, winding road descends in tight switchbacks, almost like San Francisco's famous Lombard St., to end abruptly at a stop sign.
- 23.1 Turn left at the T intersection onto unmarked Spring Valley Rd. Soon you'll pass Teatown Lake on your left.
- 23.7 Turn left into the Teatown Lake Reservation parking lot.

A Taste of New England Challenge

Bedford—Ridgefield—North Wilton—
Pound Ridge—Bedford

This ride, a somewhat abbreviated version of the 60-mile Bedford Silver Spring Sally of the Long Island Bicycle Club, Inc., is a tour of places reminiscent of New England. In fact, some of it is technically in New England, as part of the route dances back and forth across the New York border into Fairfield County, Connecticut. But most of it takes you through some of the hills in the eastern part of New York's Westchester County.

The shorter version of the ride is a brisk cruise for cyclists in moderately good condition; the roller-coaster terrain is challenging enough that the longer version should appeal to strong cyclists. The starting point in Bedford is close enough to New York City that the route can make a good one-day ride for city-dwellers who own or rent cars, but the forest is so quiet that you will be tempted to linger overnight as a momentary respite from city life.

If you want to make a weekend of it, that is easily done. You may luxuriate at a number of noted bed-and-breakfast inns in Ridgefield, Connecticut. Among them are the West Lane Inn (203–438–7323) and The Elms Inn (203–438–2541),

Ridgefield's oldest continuously functioning inn, taking in guests since 1799.

For those preferring the wide open spaces, try camping at one of Westchester County's beautiful parks. At the 4,700-acre Ward Pound Ridge Reservation 6 miles north of Bedford (914–763–3493), you can rent an open-faced lean-to cabin large enough to shelter eight sleeping bags. Farther north try one of the rustic cabins or tent sites at the 1,000-acre Mountain Lakes Campground, where some of the campsites also have showers (914–593–2618 or 669–5793).

This route, verified by Jay Carney of Madison, Connecticut, is perfect for a crisp autumn ride to gaze at the golden and fiery leaves. But please note that on nice weekends, the traffic on some stretches can be moderate to moderately heavy. Fortunately, all the main routes have paved shoulders, though the back roads do not.

The Basics

Start: Bedford, New York, at the village green (Rtes. 172 and 22). To get to the start, take exit 4 off I–684 onto Rte.172E, and follow Rte. 172E to Bedford's village green. From the Merrit Pkwy., take exit 34 and then Rte 104 north to Rte 172E to Bedford's village green.
Length: 34 or 47 miles.
Terrain: Moderately hilly to hilly. Traffic ranges from light to moderately heavy. The side roads are very narrow.
Food: Available in Bedford, New York, and Ridgefield, Connecticut, and at widely spaced convenience stores as noted; if in doubt, stock up.

Miles & Directions

■ 0.0 Head north on busy Rte. 22 (passing the Bedford Playhouse on your right immediately after leaving the village).

TWIN LAKES
VILLAGE

RIDGEFIELD

Straight for 47 mile
ride; turn right for
34-mile ride

*Entrance to
Ward Pound
Ridge Reservation*

N

NORTH
WILTON

BEDFORD

★ START/
FINISH

POUND
RIDGE

NEW YORK
(Westchester County)

(Fairfield County)
CONNECTICUT

- 0.3 Bear right at the triangle onto Rte. 121N.
- 2.0 Turn right onto Rte. 137.
- 3.0 Take the second left onto secluded Honey Hollow Rd., following it as it eventually makes a sharp left.
- 6.0 Turn right at the T intersection onto Rte. 121N. In 0.75 mile you will pass the entrance to the Ward Pound Ridge Reservation. If you ride into the park, there are public rest rooms with water in the building on your right, just before the guard's kiosk.
- 6.9 Turn right at the T intersection where Rte. 121N joins Rte. 35E. A deli and market are here.
- 7.4 Turn left at the light to stay on Rte. 121N; the gas station and deli at this intersection are the last opportunity for food or snacks until Ridgefield in another 14 miles.
- 12.0 Turn right onto Hawley Rd. at the brown sign for Mountain Lakes Camp. This road climbs continuously for the next mile.
- 13.2 Follow the road as it bends sharply left (at the brown sign for Mount Lakes Camp) and becomes unmarked Oscaleta Rd. *Caution!* The road descends quite steeply, and there may be traffic behind blind corners. In 0.3 mile on the left, pass the entrance to Mountain Lakes Camp.
- 14.5 Bear left at the Y intersection to stay on Oscaleta Rd. (Benedict Rd. heads right).
- 15.0 Turn left onto Old Oscaleta Rd. at a sign that says STOP SIGN AHEAD, just before the stop sign at Main St. Use caution on this turn and do not overshoot it. Old Oscaleta Rd. is a lovely roller-coaster ride that takes you across the border into Connecticut.
- 15.8 Turn left at the T intersection onto unmarked New Oscaleta Rd.
- 16.1 Make the first right onto Oscaleta Rd., which plunges down. (If you erroneously stay on New Oscaleta Rd., you will continue to climb.)
- 17.6 Turn right at the T intersection onto unmarked Rte. 102 (Barry Ave.), which leads into the town of Ridgefield.

- 18.7 Turn right at the T intersection to stay on Rte. 102 (High Ridge Ave.).
- 18.8 Turn left at the stop sign to stay on Rte. 102 (Catoonah St.).
- 19.1 Turn right at the light to stay on Rte. 102 (Main St.), which joins Rte. 35. Many places to eat are along this stretch. For instance, should you go left rather than right at this intersection, a gourmet hotdog stand is just 0.2 mile away. Watch carefully for auto traffic.
- 19.5 Keep heading straight on Rte. 35 where Rte. 102 turns left.
- 19.7 Keep heading straight at the fountain onto Rte. 33, where Rte. 35 (West Lane) bears right.

For the 34-mile cruise turn right at this fountain to stay on Rte. 35 (West Ln.), passing the West Lane Inn on your right. In 0.6 mile, where Silver Spring Rd. comes in from the left, pick up the directions at mile 36.0 below.

Although broken up by several rises, the next 5 miles along Rte. 33 is a net downhill. The road name changes from W. Wilton Rd. to Ridgefield Rd. at the border of Wilton Township but remains Rte. 33. The road is narrow but has a good surface; however, watch for sand. At about 5 miles, near the top of a rise, prepare to stop.

- 25.5 At the stop sign turn right onto Drum Hill Rd. Make an immediate right onto quiet, unmarked Cheese Spring Rd., which becomes Mariomi Rd. at the border of New Canaan Township.
- 28.8 Turn right at the T intersection onto Valley Rd.
- 30.1 Shortly after crossing a small concrete bridge, turn at the second right onto Benedict Hill Rd.
- 30.3 Turn left onto S. Bald Hill Rd.
- 31.1 Jog right at the T intersection onto the unmarked N. Wilton Rd., and then make an immediate left onto the narrow, one-lane N. Bald Hill Rd.

- 31.3 Bear left at the Y intersection to continue on N. Bald Hill Rd. This is a beautiful stretch. As you reenter New York State, the road becomes graded dirt with many sharp stones that could work mischief on narrow tires. Ride slowly.

- 32.2 Turn left at the T intersection onto unmarked Silver Spring Rd. Although it starts out as graded dirt, it becomes paved again as you reenter Connecticut.

- 34.6 Bear left at the Y intersection to stay on Silver Spring Rd. until it ends at busy Rte. 35. At mile 34.6, just before you reach Rte. 35, you will cross over West Lane (CT 835).

- 36.0 Turn left at the T intersection onto unmarked but busy Rte. 35 (So. Salem Rd.). This is where the 34-mile ride rejoins the 47-mile route. If you were to turn right instead, you would pass two antiques stores, a pizza/deli, and the West Lane bed-and-breakfast inn. At mile 36.7, after Rte. 35 changes names several times, you will reenter New York for the final time. At mile 36.9 keep riding straight through the light to stay on Rte. 35.

- 37.4 Turn left onto Ridgefield Ave. (Watch carefully, for it is easy to miss!) Eventually it changes its name to Highview Rd.

- 39.2 Turn left at the T intersection onto Rte. 124 (Salem-High Ridge Rd.).

- 42.0 Bear right onto Rte. 137N in Pound Ridge.

- 44.8 Turn left at the T intersection onto Rte. 121.

- 46.4 Turn left at the T intersection onto Rte. 22S.

- 46.7 You are back at the Bedford village green.

Great Finger Lakes Wineries Challenge

Watkins Glen—Ovid—Interlaken—
Reynoldsville—Burdett—Watkins Glen

The Finger Lakes are so popular for cycling that at least one publisher has devoted an entire guidebook to them for cyclists (*20 Bicycle Tours in the Finger Lakes,* by Mark Roth and Sally Walters, Backcountry Publications, Third edition, 1990).

The Finger Lakes are eleven long and narrow bodies of water gouged out by glaciers millions of years ago during the Ice Age in what is now western New York State. Seneca Lake, whose shore is hugged by the initial part of this ride, is the second largest of the lakes: 40 miles long, 4 miles wide, and so deep that its bottom is 200 feet below sea level. The southern end of Seneca Lake, where this ride takes you, is tucked between forested high hills relieved by valleys that cradle dairy farms, vineyards, and orchards. This ride begins and ends at Watkins Glen State Park (607–535–4511), which has a splendid gorge featuring rock caverns and nineteen cascading waterfalls—and an Olympic-size swimming pool for sluicing off the road grime. You can make the park your base of operations by setting up camp at one of its cabins or tent/trailer sites (Watkins Glen KOA, 607–535–7404) just 0.5 mile west of the park's lower entrance on Route 329, which is off Rte. 14.

Alternatively, if your idea of roughing it is making do with black-and-white television, you might prefer to stay in one of Watkins Glen's bed-and-breakfast inns. For a brochure listing the many lovely inns in the area, contact the Finger Lakes Association (309 Lake Street, Penn Yan, NY 14527; (315) 536–7488 or (800) KIT–4–FUN; Web site: embark.com/Finger-Lakes.

The cycling through Schuyler, Seneca, and Tompkins Counties is moderately rolling to undeniably hilly, although the traffic outside the town of Watkins Glen is generally light. As upstate New York is the largest wine-producing area in the United States outside California, this route passes a number of vineyards, all of which let visitors sample their fare. (If you do so, be sparing: Remember that cycling under the influence of alcohol is even dumber than driving while intoxicated, since you have no protection of a metal shell around you.)

The village of Ovid (mile 23), the northernmost point of the ride not quite halfway through, holds a strawberry festival the second Saturday in June. An attractive village square with surrounding stores and churches makes this town a perfect rest or lunch stop any time of the bicycling season.

This route is from the Great Finger Lakes Bicycle Tour, held annually by the Southern Tier Bicycle Club. Each May or June the two-day tour, which can be joined by any cyclist for a modest fee, features different routes; this route is the day one portion of the 1991 tour, originally devised and verified by Augie Mueller of Vestal, New York. (To join the group's annual Great Finger Lakes Bicycle Tour, contact Mueller at 607–722–6005 or via e-mail at amueller@binghamton.edu.)

The Basics

Start: Watkins Glen, at the lower entrance to Watkins Glen State Park on Rte. 14 (North Franklin St.) at Tenth St. To get to the start, take Rte. 17 to Elmira and then Rte. 14 north to

Watkins Glen. The entrance to the park is on your left after you enter Watkins Glen.

Length: 55 miles.

Terrain: Rolling to moderately hilly. Traffic is generally light except in Watkins Glen. Another plus for this region in regard to cycling are the excellent paved shoulders that extend for almost the entire tour outside the village areas.

Food: Several stores in Watkins Glen, Burdett, Trumansburg, Interlaken, and Ovid. After Trumansburg (mile 36.4), there are few opportunities to stop for food until you reach Burdett (mile 50). Soon you will have a breathtaking downhill into Watkins Glen and can stop there at Tobe's Coffee Shop and Bakery.

Miles & Directions

- 0.0 From the lower entrance to Watkins Glen State Park, head left (north) on Rte. 14 (Main St.).
- 0.4 Turn right (east) at the light onto 4th St., following Rte. 414N. In 500 feet you'll pass Tobe's Coffee Shop and Bakery.
- 2.0 Bear left to stay on Rte. 414N. Now you just cruise along for the next 21 miles, with Seneca Lake (renowned for its trout fishing) off to your left. When you first turn onto Rte. 414, the paved shoulder will be a bit skimpy. However, it improves dramatically as you cross from Schuyler into Seneca County at mile 12.
- 14.3 Along the way you'll pass a number of vineyards and wineries, the most prominent being the Wagner Vineyards/Ginny Lee Cafe (9322 Rte. 414, Lodi, NY 14860, 607–582–6574, wagwine@ptd.net or www.fingerlakes.net/wagner). Since the Ginny Lee is about an hour's cycling time from the state park, you should consider stopping either there or in the hamlets of Lodi (mile 18) or Ovid (mile 23). The view of Seneca Lake from the lakeside veranda of

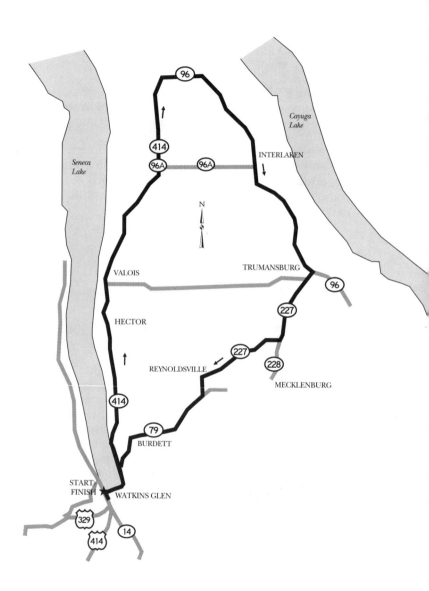

the Ginny Lee Cafe is simply stunning. Continue north on Rte. 414/96A.

- 23.0 Shortly after passing through the hamlet of Ovid, turn right (east) onto Rte. 96. Continue through the village of Interlaken (mile 31), passing Rte. 96A, and bear left a mile south of Interlaken to stay on Rte. 96.

- 36.4 Just before the village of Trumansburg, turn right onto Rte. 227. For a pleasant rest stop, continue 100 yards and visit the village, which is known locally for its unique architecture, good food, and friendly residents.

- 40.3 Turn right at Rte. 228 to stay on Rte. 227, continuing on toward Reynoldsville and Watkins Glen. At about mile 45, Rte. 227 makes a sharp turn to the left and, for the first time on this tour, the paved shoulder ends, but it picks up again less than a mile later at the intersection with NY 79.

- 46.1 Merge right onto Rte. 79W where Rte. 227 ends. After entering the village of Burdett (about mile 50), veer left to stay on Rte. 79, carefully braking on the steep downhill to Seneca Lake. Remember to check your brakes before making this descent.

- 52.2 Continue straight onto Rte. 414 as Rte. 79 ends.

- 53.8 Tobe's Coffee Shop and Bakery on your left!

- 54.0 Turn left onto Rte. 14S.

- 54.3 You are now back at the lower entrance to Watkins Glen State Park. If, by some twisted trick of fate, you are still in a hill climbing mood, you might try the hill going up to the main section of the park. That road (SR 329) is on your right, just south of Glen Creek and the entrance to the lower park.

5

St. Lawrence River Church Cruise

Canton—Morley—Madrid—
Waddington—Chipman—Canton

With 2,800 square miles, St. Lawrence County is the *fifth* largest U.S. county east of the Mississippi and the largest county in New York, equal in area to Rhode Island and Delaware combined. Its gently rolling terrain crossed by scenic roads in excellent condition with little traffic makes it a haven for cyclists; yet so few people (114,000 in 1990) live in the county that it has never really been discovered by the bicycling world. This gentle 46-mile cruise will give you a chance to sample this lovely—but rather remote—area for yourself.

Originally developed in 1991 by the author (Dale Lally) as part of the Canton, New York, Bicycle Club's preparation for GEAR 92 (a major bike rally), the St. Lawrence River Church Cruise immediately became a very popular tour for locals and visitors, novices and experienced cyclists alike, and has remained so ever since. Originally called the Church Ride, the tour passes ten beautiful and historic churches in Canton, Morley, Madrid, Waddington, and Chipman. Devoting a whole day to the ride is a good idea because even though it is only 46 miles long, your pace will be slowed by the scenery, the churches, and the eateries along the way.

The ride begins at the village park in Canton, the county seat of St. Lawrence County. Despite its remote location (the nearest major metropolitan area is Ottawa, the capital of Canada, 75 miles to the north), Canton is part of an academic oasis, home to both St. Lawrence University (whose 1,000-acre campus makes up most of the southeast side of the village) and the Canton campus of the State University of New York (SUNY). Moreover, a mere 10 miles away lies Potsdam, with Clarkson University and SUNY's Potsdam campus. What does this mean for touring cyclists? As a result of several thousand college students getting around by bicycle, local governments have become increasingly sensitive to the potential of bicycle touring.

This tour's destination, the village of Waddington on the St. Lawrence River, is worth exploring for the majestic Victorian homes that make it appear as though time has stood still since about 1890. Waddington has several excellent restaurants (some open on Sunday), antiques shops, and even a delightful hardware store (also open on Sunday). Another local attraction for sweaty cyclists is the Waddington town beach at the western edge of the village. With a covered shelter, rest rooms, and changing rooms, it's perfect for a picnic or a swim in the clear water of the St. Lawrence River. Over the past several years, the water has been cleaned up by zebra mussels, which have learned to eat everything but people!

Because Canton is so far north, the best time to visit is June through September. Snow has been known to linger on until late April, and May can be rainy and snowy. But the summer and early autumn are quite pleasant, and the tree-lined backroads around Canton and throughout the county are simply gorgeous. Those wishing to gaze at the spectacular fall foliage may prefer to try the tour in the brisk air of late September or early October, before the first snow falls. The biggest problem for cyclists in the area are the infamous black flies, which can be a pest unless you slather yourself with an effective insect repellent such as Cutter's. And keep your mouth shut while riding, or you will end up with bugs for dessert.

Canton has several motels, including the University Best Western, (315) 386–8522; the Comfort Suites, (315) 386–1161; the St. Lawrence Inn, (315) 386–8587, and the Cascade Inn, (315) 386–8503. There are also several very nice B&Bs both in the village itself and within six miles of Canton proper. In addition to the county Chamber of Commerce, B&B information may be obtained directly from the local B&B association at ostbbinn@northnet.org (315–386–2126). There are no campgrounds in the immediate Canton area but many of them, both state and private, along the nearby St. Lawrence River. For example, Cole's Creek State Campground is located just 4 miles east of Waddington on NY 37 or about 22 miles from Canton. For information or reservations for any New York state park, call the "I Love New York" toll free number at 1–800–ILOVENY. And for further information about the churches or touring in St. Lawrence County, including information on the B&Bs, contact the St. Lawrence County Chamber of Commerce, Tallman Building, Canton, NY 13617, (315) 386–4000, on the Web at www.northnet.org/slchamber; e-mail: slccoc@northnet.org.

There are two very good bicycle shops in the Canton-Potsdam area. In Canton, it's the Bicycle Post at 70 Main Street (315) 386–3756, run by John Post, an accomplished racer, on the Web at www.thebicyclepost.com, e-mail: info@thebicyclepost.com. The other shop, the Tread Mill, (315) 265–5850, is located 10 miles away in Potsdam, on the Web at www.potsdam.ny.us/thetreadmill, e-mail: treadmil@slic.com. A rather large shop stuffed with a huge stock of bicycles and accessories, the "Mill" also does a brisk mail order business.

The Basics

Start: The village square in Canton. From the south and west (the Syracuse area), take I–81 north to exit 48 just north of

Watertown. Then take Rte. 342 east for about 5 miles. Turn left (north) onto Rte. 11 for the remaining 60 or so miles to Canton. From the east (through Tupper Lake), take Rte. 3 west for about 17 miles to Sevey's Corners. At Sevey's Corners, turn right (north) onto Rte. 56 for 18 miles to Colton. At Colton, turn left (west) onto Rte. 68 for another 12 miles into Canton. Both Rte. 11 and Rte. 68 will take you directly to Canton's Main Street and the village square.

Note: The good news is that the New York State Department of Transportation has designated the entire length of U.S. Route 11—all the way from the Canadian border at Rouse's Point to the Pennsylvania border—as New York State Bike Route 11. The bad news is that, as of late 1998, the route has yet to get signs stating this.

Length: 46 miles.

Terrain: Flat to gently rolling, so sedate that even a five-speed cluster should suffice.

Food: Many choices in Canton, Madrid, and Waddington, from fast food to sit-down restaurants, although most country restaurants are closed on Sunday. Obviously, the best day to tour is on Saturday, when the stores and restaurants are sure to be open; otherwise, pack a few snacks.

Miles & Directions

- 0.0 In Canton's village square, face the Canton Free Library (Park St.) and look to your left. You will see the rather imposing First Presbyterian Church, built between 1876 and 1883 by Ogdensburg architect James Johnston in the style of Gothic parish design. Then turn right and cross Main Street, which becomes Court St.
- 0.1 Turn left onto Chapel St. and glide downhill to the three-way intersection of Riverside Drive and Chapel and State Streets.
- 0.3 Turn right onto Riverside Dr. (St. Lawrence County Rte.

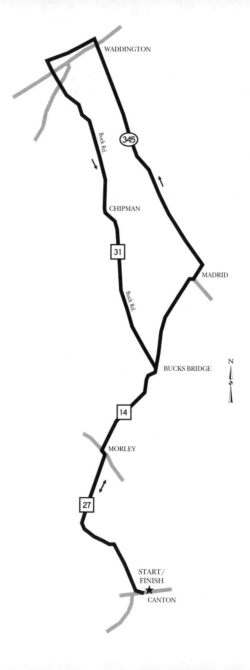

WADDINGTON

Buck Rd.

345

CHIPMAN

31

Buck Rd

MADRID

BUCKS BRIDGE

N

14

MORLEY

27

START/
FINISH

CANTON

27, abbreviated CR 27). For the next 12 miles, you will be playing tag with the Grasse River on your left up to Morley and on your right to Bucks Bridge.

- 6.1 At the intersection of CR 27 and 14 in Morley, turn left (south) onto CR 14. In about 200 yards stop, for on the left side of the road is Trinity Chapel, an exact replica of a thirteenth-century English parish church, complete with graveyard. This early Gothic revival chapel was designed by New York architect Charles C. Haight and built in 1868, but was closed in 1976 because of high maintenance costs. Now it is opened only for special occasions such as weddings. After viewing it, retrace your route back to the intersection of CR 27 and proceed straight through the intersection to continue northeast on CR 14 toward Bucks Bridge.

- 9.4 Bucks Bridge. Follow CR 14 around to the left and stop. On your left is Bucks Bridge Community Church, which appeared on the cover of the September 1992 issue of *Bicycle USA*, the magazine of the League of American Bicyclists. Bucks Bridge's second claim to fame is the historical marker to your right, next to an old stone foundation. According to local tradition, that foundation is the remains of the first Seventh-day Adventist Church. After your examination, continue straight on CR 14 toward Madrid.

- 12.8 Madrid. At the Atlantic gas station, go straight onto North St. (where CR 14 curves right). In one block on your left, at Church St., you will find Madrid's oldest and most imposing edifice, St. John the Baptist Catholic Church. (Another interesting church is the United Church, about a block away at 39 Main St.) From St. John's, turn right onto Church St. and go one block to the intersection of CR 14 and Rte. 345. That intersection is the center of the village of Madrid and features a couple of restaurants and a convenience store. Except for the Madrid Hotel the village pretty much closes down on Sunday. The hotel long ago gave up renting rooms, so don't even ask. It has a bar but the real draw for touring cyclists is the restaurant. Unfortunately, it is only open until noon on Sunday. In case the restaurant is closed at the time you arrive, there are several food and snack possibilities in Waddington, which is just nine miles farther.

■ 13.0 At the main intersection in Madrid, turn left onto the combined CR 14/Rte. 345.

■ 13.6 Bear left to follow Rte. 345. (CR 14 continues straight.)

■ 22.8 Waddington. At the blinking light (the only traffic light in Waddington) at the intersection with Rte. 37, stop and look immediately to your right to see St. Paul's Episcopal Church. Built in 1818, it is the oldest stone church in northern New York. Just a block beyond stands St. Mary's Roman Catholic Church, built first in 1854 and rebuilt in 1924, retaining the original walls and foundation. Just beyond St. Mary's is a third "bonus" church, the First Presbyterian Church, dating from about 1887. According to an undocumented local tradition, it was built by Isaac Johnson, a former slave from Kentucky who lived in Ontario and St. Lawrence County and distinguished himself by building a number of bridges and churches. After examining these churches, continue north another 2 blocks on Rte. 345 to the St. Lawrence River.

■ 23.0 Turn left onto St. Lawrence Ave. In about 2 miles, the Waddington town beach will be on your right. After a picnic and a dip, turn left from the beach to retrace your route about 50 yards back to the very first intersection, which is Buck Rd.

■ 24.2 Turn right (south) onto Buck Rd., crossing Rte. 37 (at mile 24.6) and CR 28 (at mile 25.1).

■ 26.2 Continue straight at the stop sign onto CR 33 (which is still Buck Rd. but is not marked). Get ready for the most scenic part of the whole tour! For the next 10 miles, Buck Rd. is in generally good condition, and, with shade trees, a lightly rolling terrain, babbling brooks, and very few cars, this segment is absolutely superb. At mile 30.8, you'll reach Chipman, home of the final ecclesiastical jewel on this tour: a beautiful Scottish Presbyterian church on the right side of the road just north of the intersection with CR 31. In the late eighteenth and early nineteenth centuries, this area was settled by a group of Scottish immigrant dairy farmers, who formed a congregation early on. Although the current Chipman church dates only from the 1890s , several of the older original stone homes have survived to this day. If possible, go inside the church and check out the wood inlay interior. After leaving the church, turn right to continue south on CR 33 (Buck Rd.) for another few yards.

- 30.9 Turn left onto CR 31.
- 31.3 Turn right onto the continuation of Buck Rd.
- 36.5 Turn right onto unmarked CR 14. You may notice that you are back at Bucks Bridge Community Church, which you passed earlier in the day. Follow CR 14 around to the right and continue back to Morley.
- 39.3 At Morley, turn left (south) onto CR 27.
- 45.4 Canton. Turn left onto Main St. (U.S. Rte. 11) and ride up the hill to the village square.
- 45.6 Arrive at the village square.

Note: To see more of the picturesque village of Canton, visit the Canton Free Library on Park St. in the village square and ask for the brochure describing the village walking and cycling tours.

6

Cannonsville Reservoir All-Class Challenge

Deposit—Walton—Trout Creek—Deposit

The names Ashokan, Cannonsville, Cross River, Hemlock, Kensico, Neversink, New Croton, Pepacton, and Roundout may not mean much to the average New York City resident, but these are some of the many reservoirs that assure the Big Apple of having some of the best drinking water in the world. These far-off locations are all patrolled by the New York City Police Department, and to fish in the reservoirs that allow it, one needs a special permit issued by New York City. One of the farthest from the city—a good 150 miles—is the Cannonsville Reservoir on the West Branch of the Delaware River in Delaware County. This ride around it is one of three in this book contributed and/or verified by Augie Mueller (amueller@binghamton.edu) of Vestal, New York.

The 10-mile-long section along Route 206 between Walton and Trout Creek is undeniably hilly; the whole route ridden as the loop described here should appeal to cyclists in excellent condition who do not mind busy car traffic. (For a challenge that's 1.3 miles shorter with somewhat less traffic, take Delaware County Route 47 from Route 206, bypassing Trout Creek; although the surface is less smooth than the main route, it is a quiet, pretty road that is a nice downhill.) The many parking areas along Route 10, however, allow this rather sedate 54-mile challenge to be customized for all riding levels, great for a club or family ride. The trip along Route 10 from Deposit to Walton is gently rolling terrain, always near water, with light traffic and good shoulders; an out-and-back round-trip just between these two towns is 52 relatively flat miles. That cruise can be made as short as 35 miles by starting from the junction of State Route 10 and County Route 27. More-over, the 8.4-mile section between the junction of Routes 10 and 27 and Trout Creek is also "extremely rewarding, with the babbling of the creek and vistas of sharp hills adding to the enjoyment of gliding down the extra-smooth, quiet valley road," notes Mueller. A round-trip of this stretch makes a good ramble of 17 miles. For a longer cruise, join the ramble and the shorter cruise together: Start from the junction and ride to both Walton and Trout Creek along Routes 10 and 27, retracing your path for a total round-trip of 52 miles. Everyone has a great time without getting lost and can talk about much of the same scenery. Every season has its unique beauty, but in Mueller's opinion, "early spring (May and June) with the water high and trees greening competes with the fantastic fall colors" (late September and all of October).

The Basics

Start: The intersection of Division St. and Hwy. 10 in Deposit, New York, 25 miles east of Binghamton. From New York State Rte. 17, the Southern Tier Expressway, take exit 84 onto Rtes. 8 and 10 north to Deposit, less than a mile off the highway. Park anywhere in Deposit or along Rte. 10.
Length: 54 miles (the full loop) or anything shorter (17, 35, or 52 miles), depending on how you customize the ride.
Terrain: Level to gently rolling between Deposit and Walton and between Deposit and Trout Creek, with light traffic. Rte. 206 between Walton and Trout Creek, however, is quite hilly and can also be busy.
Food: Deposit and Walton both have good restaurants and

groceries. Trout Creek has a convenience store. No other services are along the route, so pack all the water, food, and tools you may need. *Note:* On Sundays from May 1 to October 30, from 8:00 A.M.. to 1:00 P.M., various groups serve a pancake breakfast for a few dollars at the White Birch Airfield, a grass-strip airport 3.2 miles off State Rte. 10 up Sand Creek Rd. (County Rte. 67). It is a tough, steep climb on a bicycle, but one could drive there and then leave the car on Rte. 10 near Sand Creek Rd. Once you are on Sand Creek Rd., signs clearly mark the way to the airport.

Miles & Directions

- 0.0 Leave Deposit on Rte. 10N.
- 1.6 Turn right to stay on Rte. 10 at the junction of Rtes. 10, 8, and 48. At mile 7.7, you will pass Sand Creek Rd. on your right (heading toward the White Birch Airfield with its Sunday pancake breakfasts).
- 8.5 Just after crossing over the reservoir, bear right at the Y intersection to stay on Rte. 10 where County Rte. 27 (with a sign to Trout Creek) comes in from the left. You will pass over the West Branch of the Delaware River several times in the next 10 or 12 miles. At mile 21.0, look to your left to see the Beerston District Police Division headquarters of the New York City Police Department. Pass Beers Brook Rd. on your right 0.1 mile later; although it looks inviting, it leads to the land of regrets—huge hills and unpaved roads. Stay on Rte. 10. Beers Brook Rd. is a convenient landmark, though, heralding the next turn 0.1 mile later.
- 21.2 Turn right onto South River Rd.
- 26.0 Turn left onto Rte. 206, cross the river again, and enter Walton. Barely a tenth of a mile later, turn left onto Walton's main street, Delaware St., which is also Routes 10 and 206. Traffic could be heavy in this area.
- 26.5 At the Hess gas station turn right onto West St. After passing the Agway, the Walton Dollar Bazaar, and the fire-

WALTON

BEERSTON

S. River Rd.

206

LOOMIS

N

TROUT
CREEK

27

10

START/
FINISH
DEPOSIT

house, West St. becomes Lower Third Brook Rd. and eventually plain old Third Brook Rd.

- 28.2 Bear left at the fork to stay on Third Brook Rd. (where Seeley Wood Rd. breaks off to the right).
- 28.6 Bear right onto Rte. 206, but watch for traffic. At mile 32.7 you will pass the left turn for CR 47 (Loomis Brook Rd.) should you wish to slightly shorten your return by by-passing Trout Creek (and the only remaining convenience store on the route).
- 36.2 Trout Creek. Turn left onto CR 27. At mile 39.2 you will pass the terminus of Rte. 47 coming in from the left.
- 44.7 Turn right onto Rte. 10.
- 51.6 Left at the stop sign to remain on Rte. 10.
- 53.7 Enter downtown Deposit.

7

Skaneateles Lake Cruise

*Skaneateles—Borodino—
Scott—New Hope—Skaneateles*

Hill-climbers who love rural areas are certain to enjoy this rolling and scenic route circling Skaneateles (pronounced "skinny atlas") Lake. The second easternmost of the eleven Finger Lakes, Skaneateles Lake offers lovely vistas of sailboats, as well as fishing and swimming. The Lightning class sailboat was developed on its waters, and today the lake hosts many races and regattas. The lake also supports one of the few remaining water-borne mail delivery routes, which leaves Skaneateles every day at 10:00 A.M. For a modest fare you can catch it for a three-hour tour. Call Mid-Lakes Navigation at (315) 685–8500.

This ride, verified by author Dale Lally of the Canton, New York, Bicycle Club, was originally contributed by Peter C. Lemonides, cartographer for the Onondaga Cycling Club of Syracuse, New York. It begins in the town of Skaneateles and passes through Onondaga, Cortland, and Cayuga Counties. The town, which calls itself the Eastern Gateway to the Finger Lakes, has many wonderful nineteenth-century buildings, along with some world-class (and expensive) restaurants. Of local fame is Krebs (founded in 1899), which serves family-style dinners and a Sunday brunch. However, do not look for a bike shop in Skaneateles. The closest is in Auburn, seven miles west on Route 20.

If you wish to stay overnight, you can rest your bones at

the Sherwood Inn (315) 885–3405, which you will pass near the end of the route. Its sixteen guest rooms are decorated in a variety of nineteenth-century styles. A stay at the inn, which traces its origin to a building that fed and housed travelers on Isaac Sherwood's stagecoach line as long ago as 1807, includes a continental breakfast.

The Basics

Start: At the Skaneateles municipal parking lot on Rte. 321 (State St.) just off Rte. 20 (Genesee St.). From the Syracuse area take I–81 south to exit 15 and then Rte. 20W into Skaneateles.
Length: 46.3 miles.
Terrain: Hilly. Heavy traffic on NY 20, light on Rte. 41, and very light on the rest of the roads.
Food: Readily available in Skaneateles but sparse elsewhere, so pack a lunch and snacks.

Miles & Directions

- 0.0 Turn right out of the municipal parking lot onto Rte. 321 (State St.).
- 0.1 Turn left (east) onto Rte. 20 (Genesee St.).
- 0.6 Turn right (south) onto Rte. 41S (E. Lake Rd.). Now just lay back and enjoy your up-and-down cruise along the eastern shore of Skaneateles Lake for the next 19 miles. At mile 8.4 you'll pass through the hamlet of Borodino.
- 19.5 In the hamlet of Scott, turn right onto Glen Haven Rd. Enjoy this downhill for you will have a payback in a few short miles. At about mile 20, remain on Glen Haven Rd., which makes a sharp turn to the right.
- 22.5 Turn left to stay on Glen Haven Rd. and begin climbing a big, long hill. At mile 28.5 in the town of New Hope, continue straight where the route crosses NY 41A and changes its name to New Hope Rd.

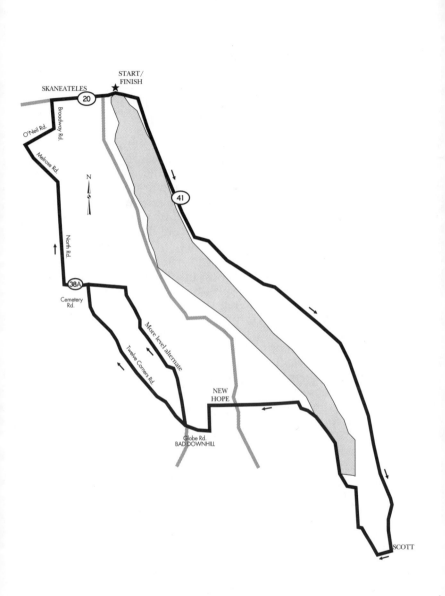

START/
FINISH

SKANEATELES

20

O'Neil Rd.

Broadway Rd.

Melrose Rd.

41

N

North Rd.

38A

Cemetery
Rd.

More level alternate

Twelve Corners Rd.

NEW
HOPE

Globe Rd.
BAD DOWNHILL

SCOTT

- 29.5 Turn left onto Old Salt Rd.
- 30.3 In the village of Kellogsville turn right onto Globe Rd. CAUTION: CHECK YOUR BRAKES! CHECK YOUR BRAKES! CHECK YOUR BRAKES! At this point you will commence a *very* steep downhill, with, naturally, a stop sign right at the bottom (mile 31.2), where Globe Rd. intersects NY 38A. After crossing Rte. 38A, the road changes its name to Twelve Corners Rd. Before proceeding a single inch through the intersection of Globe Rd. and NY 38A, consider this: Should you need a respite from the hills, you will *not* get it if you continue on Twelve Corners Rd. The hills that you just descended will extract a payback on the other side. However, you can avoid this unpleasantness by turning right (north) onto a rather flat Rte. 38A, which offers a very nice shoulder. This will add a mere 0.6 mile to the length of the tour. And this minuscule distance pales in comparison to the height of the hill you must climb should you choose to remain on Twelve Corners Rd.
- 36.5 Bear right onto unmarked Cemetery Rd., where Twelve Corners Rd. bears left.
- 37.2 Turn left onto Rte. 38A.
- 38.1 Turn right onto North Rd. *Note:* If you need a snack, there is a small convenience store just to the left (south) of the intersection of North Rd. and Rte. 38A. However, from this point you have only 7 more miles (and no big hills) to the end of the tour.
- 41.5 In the hamlet of Baptist Corner, turn left onto Melrose Rd.
- 43.3 Turn right onto O'Neil Rd.
- 44.4 Turn left at the next intersection onto unmarked (but nicely paved) Broadway Rd.
- 45.4 Turn right onto Rte. 20E (Genesee St.). Traffic will pick up considerably at this point. However, there is a fine, wide paved shoulder to ride on. Soon you'll pass Krebs and the Sherwood Inn.
- 46.2 Turn left onto Rte. 321 (State St.).
- 46.3 Turn left into the municipal parking lot.

8

Pratts Falls Half-Century-Plus Challenge

Pompey—Truxton—Erieville—Fabius—Pompey

Light traffic, hills, farms, hills, quaint villages, and more hills combine to make the Pratts Falls Half-Century-Plus a pleasant yet challenging day's ride. Passing through Onondaga and Madison Counties, this ride is a real retreat from automobiles and people:

Rolling acres of farms and four-corner towns don't offer much to tourists seeking typical tourist attractions, but they will refresh the spirit of a cyclist seeking solitude and good, scenic, challenging terrain.

The Pratts Falls Challenge was verified by Mike Rosanio of Manlius, New York. It begins at Pratts Falls Park, a county-run recreational park offering plenty of parking, covered picnic areas, rest rooms, hiking trails, and a beautiful view of Pratts Falls. (Swimming and overnight camping are not permitted.) The first opportunity to pick up provisions for the road is in the village of Pompey, 3 miles into the ride.

Beginning about 10 miles into the ride, you will be pedaling along Route 91 as it passes through the exceptionally scenic Labrador Hollow and the Labrador Mountain Ski Center. A natural lunch stop is DeRuyter, nearly halfway (26 miles) into the 58-mile loop. DeRuyter is a quaint village dotted with charming bungalows (one of which is an antique shop). You will have your choice of groceries, several small restaurants, and an ice cream parlor. Three-quarters of the way through the ride is another nice stop: Highland Forest, a county park with picnic areas, hiking trails, bridle paths, and some challenging mountain-bike trails.

The Basics

Start: Three miles north of Pompey, at Pratts Falls Park on Pratts Falls Rd. Take I–81 to exit 15 just south of Syracuse and follow Rte. 20E into Pompey. Take Henneberry Rd. north to Pratts Falls Rd. and then turn right to the park entrance.
Length: 58 miles.
Terrain: Rolling to very hilly in stretches. Traffic is light in the villages of Pompey and Fabius and extremely light everywhere else. The Rte. 13 connecting road has a lot of high-speed traffic but also smooth, wide shoulders.
Food: Occasional convenience stores and neighborhood bar-and-grill restaurants, with some long stretches in between.

Miles & Directions

- 0.0 From Pratts Falls Park parking lot, turn right onto Pratts Falls Rd.
- 0.6 At the T intersection, turn right onto Henneberry Rd., and 0.1 mile later make an immediate left to stay on Pratts Falls Rd.
- 1.3 Turn left onto Sweet Rd.
- 3.5 In the town of Pompey, bear right at the stop sign onto (unsigned) Cherry St. In 1 block cross Rte. 20 and continue straight onto Berwyn Rd.
- 5.8 Bear right onto Collins Rd. At mile 9.4 continue straight as the road becomes Berry Rd.
- 9.6 In the village of Apulia, turn left at the T intersection onto Rte. 80.

START /
FINISH

Pratts Falls Park

POMPEY

114

249

APULIA

91

TRUXTON

13

N

NEW WOODSTOCK

52

ERIEVILLE

- 9.9 Turn right onto Rte. 91. There is a 2-mile climb at mile 13.2 and another at mile 18.2 just before reaching the town of Truxton.
- 18.3 In the town of Truxton, turn left at the T intersection onto Rte. 13. At mile 22.7 continue on Rte. 13 through Cuyler.
- 26.6 In the town of DeRuyter, turn left to stay on Rte. 13.
- 31.8 In Sheds continue straight onto Dugway Rd. (where Rte. 80E heads right and Rtes. 13W/80W head left).
- 37.0 Turn left at the T intersection onto Erieville Rd.
- 37.4 In Erieville turn left at the post office onto Damon Rd. Now you begin climbing.
- 43.1 In New Woodstock continue straight onto Rte. 80W. (Rtes. 13E/80E head left and Rte. 13W heads right.) In a few miles you'll pass Highland Forest on your left.
- 50.2 In Fabius turn right onto Rte. 91.
- 55.3 In Pompey turn right onto Rte. 20.
- 55.5 Turn left onto Henneberry Rd.
- 57.5 Turn right onto Pratts Falls Rd.
- 58.1 Turn left into Pratts Falls Park.

9

Salmon River Cruise

Altmar—Orwell—Redfield—Ricard—Altmar

The rural countryside of this ride is known primarily for its hunting and fishing. You'll pedal over green rolling hills troubled by few cars, catch isolated glimpses of the reservoir, and pass many spots tempting you to stop and picnic and let your spirit catch up to your body. Although there are no bed-and-breakfast inns or campgrounds in the immediate Altmar area, there are fishing lodges available. Just 4 miles northwest on Route 13, Pulaski, which modestly bills itself as the salmon capital of the world, offers plenty of accommodations and restaurants. So if you enjoy fishing or swimming as well as cycling, this is definitely the tour for bringing your rod and reel or swimsuit. You may also want to pack your own picnic lunch before embarking, as the only food stops along the route are convenience stores in the hamlets of Altmar, Orwell, and Redfield.

This Oswego County ride begins in Altmar. The town's main attraction is the large Salmon River Fish Hatchery (315–298–5051), which offers informative tours. Perhaps the most scenic spot is 1.4 miles off the route 4.9 miles into the ride. If you turn right onto Falls Road, 1.4 miles (and a good climb) later, you will be rewarded with the sight of the Salmon River Falls, which have a greater vertical drop than Niagara Falls. Pull into the roadside parking area and hike through the woods for about 100 yards along the path. Obviously, you will hear the falls long before you see them. To see the falls at their best, visit in early spring when the river is swollen with runoff from the winter's snows. But even in the drier summer, the sight of the narrow pencil of water plummeting into the gorge below is dramatic. After viewing the falls, it will be necessary to retrace your route back out to CR 22 (and down the big hill!) where you will turn right to continue the tour.

The Basics

Start: Altmar, at the public parking lot near the Salmon River at the intersection of Bridge St. and Pulaski St. Altmar has two bars, a gas station, and a convenience store/grocery. To get to the start, take exit 36 at Pulaski off I–81 north of Syracuse, and then take Rte. 13 southeast for four miles to Altmar.
Length: 37 miles.
Terrain: Definitely hilly, particularly the 1.4-mile side trip on Falls Rd. should you choose to visit the waterfalls. There is a rather short but severe downhill 33 miles into the tour, where Rte. 30 joins Rte. 22. Your brakes should be in top condition for this tour. Traffic is very light and reasonably polite, if moving at somewhat above the posted speed limits.
Food: With convenience stores in Attmar, Orwell, and Redfield and several bars, the food situation is rather sparse. Therefore, take plenty of water and snacks along.

Miles & Directions

■ 0.0 From the public parking lot, ride away from the river up the hill along Bridge St. Three blocks later, at the T intersection, turn left onto Cemetery St., which becomes Rte. 22 at 1.3 miles into the tour. There is a Stewarts convenience store just to the right of the intersection of Bridge and Cemetery Streets.

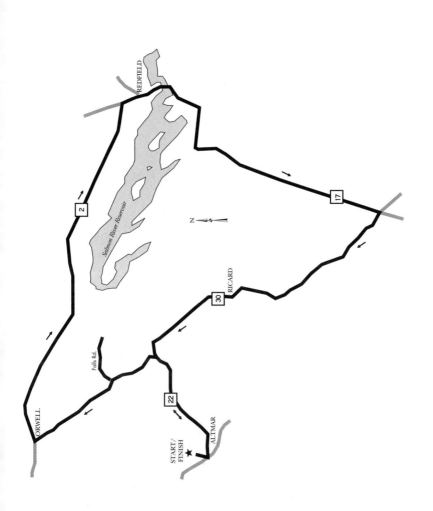

- 3.6 This is the intersection of Rtes. 30 and 22. On your in-bound leg you will be coming down the steep hill on Rte. 30 from your right. For now, however, bear left to stay on Rte. 22. In a short distance you'll cross over the Salmon River, although unfortunately you will not be able to see much of it. At mile 4.9 Falls Rd. heads right to a view of the high waterfall. This will involve 2.8 added round-trip miles, the first of which will be a rather steep hill.

- 7.5 In the rural village of Orwell, turn right onto Rte. 2, and stay on it for the next 9 miles. Eventually you will pass the Salmon River Reservoir, although it will remain mostly unseen behind the trees. You may also want to stop for a swim.

- 16.6 Intersection of Rtes. 2 and 17. Upon reaching here, glance left and you will see the Redfield Country Motel (POB 146, Redfield, NY 13437, 315–599–7222). Owner Helen Puliatti has offered the use of her facilities and to fill water bottles for touring cyclists. Eventually, however, you will be turning right and passing through the little hamlet of Redfield in less than half a mile.

- 18.2 Turn right to stay on Rte. 17.

- 19.2 Turn right to stay on Rte. 17.

- 25.4 Turn right onto C-C Rd. (A historical note: C-C Rd. was originally C.C.C. Rd., named after the Civilian Conser-vation Corps' camp there during the 1930s; somewhere along the way, the last C was dropped.) Remain alert for logging trucks. After about a mile or so, you will encounter a rather substantial logging operation on your left.

- 28.3 Turn right at the T intersection onto Rte. 30. The next 5 miles are rather flat and particularly scenic.

- 33.4 You will encounter a severe downhill and, naturally, a stop sign at a T intersection right at the bottom where Rte. 30 joins Rte. 22. Bear left onto Rte. 22. You are now retrac-ing your outbound route back into Altmar.

- 36.8 Follow Cemetery St. as it turns right onto Bridge St. Continue straight for another 3 blocks to return to the public parking lot.

10

The South Colton Four

While Canton, being home to the Canton Bicycle Club, may rightfully lay claim to being the major cycling hub of St. Lawrence County, the hamlet of South Colton, 18 miles away, has plenty to offer to touring cyclists. Directly astride Highway 56 about 6 miles south of Colton, New York, South Colton literally has everything going for it: 1) bicycle tours along scenic roads with little traffic; 2) Higley Flow State Park with camping, boating, and mountain bike trails; 3) restaurants; and 4) several bed-and-breakfasts. Of the four South Colton tours in this book, South Colton tour 1, the Gulf Road Loop, is a result of discussions with local South Colton riders. South Colton tours 2 and 3 were developed by the Canton Bicycle Club in preparation for the Great Eastern Rallies (GEARs) 1992 and 1997 sponsored by the League of American Bicyclists. (They have retained their popularity to this day.) South Colton tour 4 is a variant of the club's classic Adirondack Century, which loops from Canton to Cranberry Lake and back.

The Basics

Start: All the South Colton tours begin at the same intersection of NY 56 and Cold Brook Rd. To get to the start from the east (Lake Placid), take NY 86 9 miles to Saranac Lake. Then take NY 330 west for 21 miles to Tupper Lake. From there it's NY 3 west for 17 miles to NY 56 (Sevey Corners). From that intersection it is a mere 18 miles north on NY 56 to South Colton.

From the north (Massena) take NY 56 south for 37 miles. You will pass through a number of small communities such as Potsdam, Hannawa Falls, and Colton. Upon reaching South Colton continue through the hamlet and cross the Raquette River. The starting intersection will be the very first corner after the bridge.

From the south (Watertown) take US 11 north for 62 miles to Canton. Then take NY 68 east for 12 miles to Colton. Then take NY 56 south for 4 miles to South Colton. There is ample parking throughout the village.

By the way, the starting intesection is just a few steps away from the Braeside Bed & Breakfast (20 A Cold Brook Rd., South Colton, NY 13687, 315–262–2553). Joann Ferris is the owner and an enthusiastic member of the Canton Bicycle Club. She does everything she can for cyclists, including letting visitors park their cars on her property while doing the tours.

It should be noted that NY 56 is a great cycling route in and of itself. Starting in the St. Lawrence River community of Massena and stretching for more than 50 miles into the Adirondacks to end at the junction with NY 3, lightly traveled NY 56 offers a fine, paved shoulder; almost every inch of it is scenic path, from the flat terrain of the St. Lawrence River Valley to the Adirondacks. The one exception is a stretch of about 100 yards on a sharp curve less than 2 miles south of South Colton, where the road was cut into the side of a hill.

Caution: South Colton tours 2, 3, and 4 are not for the faint of heart or the occasional rider who must normally wait for help in case of a breakdown. In addition to requiring food and extra water, the nature of this remote region, with lots of forests and very few people, means the touring cyclist should take along tools to repair the bicycle and should know how to use them. You will not find a gas station or convenience store, much less a bicycle store, every few miles.

Terrain: On a scale of one to five with five being the hilliest, the Joe Indian Loop Challenge (Tour 3) would rate a definite four. The Rocky Mountains it is not, but the entire area is one hill after another. Even the short Gulf Road Loop (Tour 1) has a rather long but not overly steep climb. Along the Three Falls Loop Cruise (Tour 2) you will encounter a series of medium sized hills. On the Joe Indian Loop Challenge you will encounter the same series of medium hills followed by one stretch of at least 10 miles of constant climbing shortly after you turn onto Joe Indian Rd. This will be followed, however, by a screaming downhill as you enter Parishville. The hills on the Joe Indian Loop Challenge will continue all the way to just before South Colton. On the 60-plus mile Adirondack Classic (Tour 4), you will be climbing rather steadily for the first 18 miles to the intersection with NY 3. The next hilly stretch will be along Tooley Pond Rd. all the way to DeGrasse. CR 27 is rather sedate from DeGrasse north to its intersection with CR 24 at the Turnpike Tavern. From that point on, however, the hills return.

Food: Since this is a rather backwoods area, really good restaurants are rather few and far between. This is not to say there are none, just that the rather sparse population will not support a large number of them. Having said that, however, three of the four South Colton tours take you by at least one good restaurant, but there will probably be just one and not dozens as is the case downstate.

On the Gulf Road Loop, my first choice remains Lorna's Higley Diner in Colton. For the Three Falls Loop, forget any thought of buying anything along the route. It is 18 miles of pure boondocks. The Adirondack Classic has the most food opportunities, with a couple of convenience stores and at least one real restaurant, the Cranberry Lake Inn. The absolute best food in the area, however, can be had on the Joe Indian Challenge, namely the Reflections restaurant in Parishville. The downside of this is that Reflections is always closed on Monday and Tuesday and does not open until 4:00 P.M. Wednesday through Saturday. On Sunday they are open from 7:00 A.M. until 8:00 P.M., making Sunday the day of choice if you want a meal while riding the Joe Indian Challenge.

As stated elsewhere, when cycling in this part of New York,

one should always bring along plenty of water and emergency snacks. Another handy item for the handlebar bag is some sort of dog repellent.

South Colton Tour 1: Gulf Road Loop Ramble

Length: 12 miles

Miles & Directions

- 0.0 From the intersection pedal west onto Cold Brook Rd.
- 2.0 You will pass the entrance to Higley Flow State Park, a very popular park with a swimming beach, campsites, and even some cross-country ski and hiking trails.
- 3.15 Turn right (north) onto Gulf Rd. At about the 5-mile mark, you will start a rather substantial downhill. At mile 5.2 be prepared for a sharp turn to the left once you have reached the bottom. Stay on Gulf Rd. as it bears sharply left. Cottage Rd. continues on straight. If you miss this turn you will end up at a dead-end in the boondocks!
- 7.0 Lorna's Higley Diner is on your left. Worth a stop.
- 7.3 This is a three-way intersection with Gulf Rd., NY 68, and NY 56. There is also a Mobil station/convenience store at this intersection. To return to return to South Colton bear right onto southbound NY 56 for about 4 miles. Otherwise turn left onto northbound 56 and visit the hamlet of Colton, just a few hundred feet away. With a nice 4-foot shoulder and great scenery, NY 56 is a very good road to cycle in all directions. It is definitely not flat, but you will not have far to go to get back to your starting point in South Colton.
- 11.7 Return to starting point.

South Colton Tour 2: Three Falls Loop Cruise

Length: 17 miles.

Miles & Directions

- 0.0 Begin by cycling southbound (away from South Colton) on NY 56.
- 1.2 Here you will encounter two very sharp turns and the only location along the entire length of NY 56 where the shoulder almost completely disappears. Traffic is slowed to about 15 mph, and drivers can see a bit more around the curve while going in this (southerly) direction. This curve is also the reason for taking this tour in a counterclockwise direction, since the visibility around the northbound curve is almost less than zero. Regardless of which direction you are traveling, this stretch of road (about 100 yards at the maximum in either direction) demands your complete and undivided attention.
- 6.0 Left onto Stark Rd.
- 7.0 Left onto Raquette River Rd.
- 13.0 The Rainbow Falls reservoir dam will pop into view on your right. There are also several very nice picnic sites along this route. Just beyond the Rainbow Falls dam, the road designation changes from Raquette River Rd. to Three Falls Rd. Just continue on since this is the *only* road that will take you back to your starting point (or anywhere else for that matter!).
- 17.4 You will bump into Snell Rd. for just a few yards. Turn right onto Snell and you will be back at your starting point.

South Colton Tour 1: Gulf Road Loop

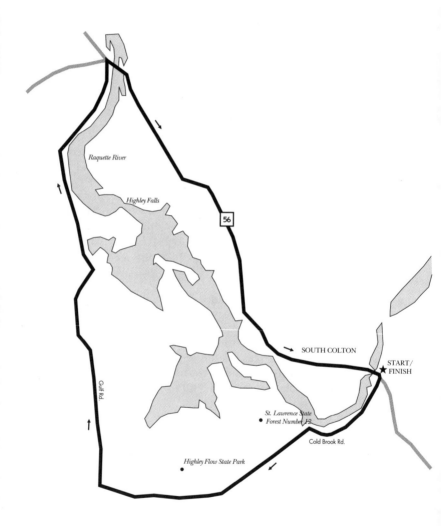

Raquette River

Highley Falls

56

Gulf Rd.

SOUTH COLTON

START/
FINISH

St. Lawrence State
Forest Number 12

Cold Brook Rd.

Highley Flow State Park

South Colton Tour 2: Three Falls Loop Cruise

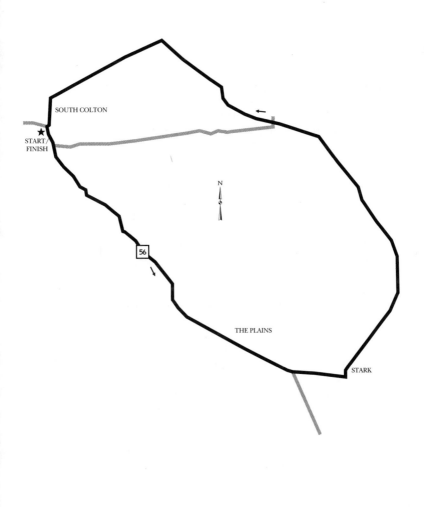

SOUTH COLTON

START/
FINISH

N

56

THE PLAINS

STARK

South Colton Tour 3: The Joe Indian Loop Challenge
(could also be called the Boondocks Loop, since you will find your-self truly out in the boonies for about 25 miles!)

Length: 43 (very tough) miles.

Miles & Directions

- 0.0 Begin cycling right across NY 56 onto Snell Rd. for about 40 feet and then turn left onto Raquette River Rd. where you will stay for the next 10 miles.
- 10.4 Turn left onto Stark Rd., which will turn into Joe Indian Rd. about half a mile later at the intersection with Carry Falls Rd. Stay on Joe Indian Rd.
- 21.1 At the intersection with Jones Rd. (to the right), Joe Indian Rd. ends and becomes White Hill Rd., named after—what else—White Hill. Remain on White Hill Rd. into Parishville. At the bottom of the hill, the road becomes George St. as it enters Parishville.
- 25.3 As you come flying down White Hill, be sure to look for the sign to the Reflections restaurant on your right. Hidden away in the woods, with a glorious view of the Raquette River, Reflections is truly a jewel in the forest. It is run by the former head cook at SUNY Potsdam, who makes all his own pastries. In addition to serving great food, the restaurant has very, very reasonable prices. At 25 miles into this tour, it's a perfect place to stop for lunch or dinner. When you leave, turn right and continue northbound on George St.
- 26.7 Turn left (west) onto CR 72 for 1 mile. Get ready for a great view of the valley off to your right and a nice downhill.
- 27.6 Approaching your next turn, note the faded blue building on your right. This is the home of the Sun Feather Soap Company (1551 Hwy 72, Potsdam, NY 13676, 315–265–3648). On the Web at www.sunsoap.com.

- 27.7 Turn right (northeast) onto the Old Potsdam–Parishville Rd.
- 30.7 Turn left (south)\onto Sinclair Rd.
- 31.7 Sinclair Rd. ends at CR 72. Jog right and then left onto Ashton Rd.
- 32.2 At the Y intersection, Pumpkin Hill Rd. will drop off to your right. However, remain left on Ashton Rd. At the third house on the left you will encounter another little North Country jewel in the woods, the Birchbark Bookstore (40 Ashton Rd., Potsdam NY 13676, 315–265–3875). Originally located in a barn with dirt floors, the current location offers thousands of used and rare books.

  Turn left (south) when coming out of Birchbark. At this point the route becomes hillier and remains so for the remaining 10 miles back to South Colton.

- 33.2 Turn right onto CR 58.
- 38.5 Turn left onto NY 56.
- 42.4 Return to starting point in South Colton.

South Colton Tour 4: The Adirondack Classic

Length: 66 miles.

Miles & Directions

- 0.0 Start cycling southbound on NY 56, and keep cycling.
- 18.0 Turn right (west) onto NY 3 for about 9 miles to Cranberry Lake. FLASH: A new convenience store, Ham's Mini Mart, has recently opened at the intersection of NY 56 and 3, open every day of the week!
- 26.0 Pass through Cranberry Lake, the last civilization until you reach DeGrasse (mile 43). It is imperative that you refuel and replenish at Cranberry Lake before tackling

South Colton Tour 3: The Joe Indian Loop Challenge

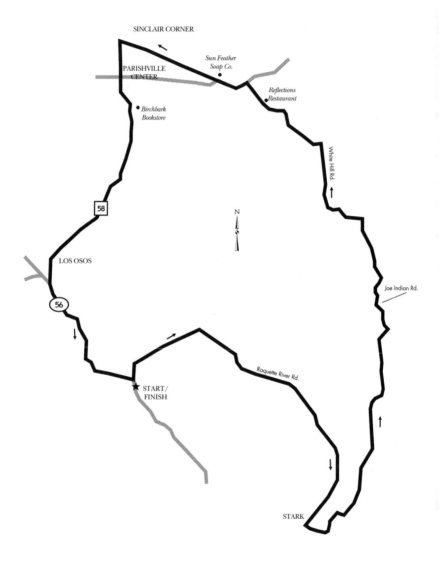

SINCLAIR CORNER

*Sun Feather
Soap Co.*

PARISHVILLE
CENTER

*Reflections
Restaurant*

● *Birchbark
Bookstore*

White Hill Rd.

58

N

LOS OSOS

Joe Indian Rd.

56

Raquette River Rd.

★ START/
FINISH

STARK

South Colton Tour 4: The Adirondack Classic

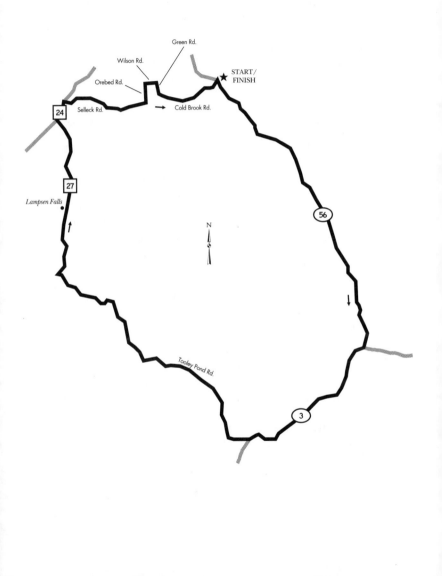

Green Rd.

Wilson Rd.

Orebed Rd.

START/
FINISH

24

Selleck Rd.

Cold Brook Rd.

27

Lampsen Falls

N

56

Tooley Pond Rd.

3

one of the prettiest (mostly) paved roads known to North Country cyclists: Tooley Pond Rd.

- 27.0 Less than a mile west of Cranberry Lake, turn right (north) onto Tooley Pond Rd. Just at 16 miles long between Cranberry Lake and DeGrasse, Tooley Pond Rd. offers some of the finest cycling in the Adirondacks—and it is almost totally paved. For some strange reason there are about ten short stretches of hard-packed dirt, each about 300 yards long, along its entire length. Nevertheless, many cyclists on narrow, high pressure tires have gone the distance of Tooley Pond Rd. and survived. Being a rather deserted backroad in the Adirondacks, there are quite a few ups and downs, so check your brakes before departure. Also check your camera, since it is not unusual to encounter all sorts of wildlife along this road. Another caveat: Do not do this stretch alone. If you run into mechanical trouble, it could be some time before anyone comes along to help, and it's a long, lonely hike back to civilization. This is so far out in the country that even your cell phone might be useless.

- 43.0 Before heading north (right) onto CR 27, I suggest you turn left and cross the bridge into downtown DeGrasse where you should find at least one convenience store, and possibly two, open on Sunday. Replenish your water and snacks, for there will be a fantastic picnic opportunity at Lampsen Falls, just a few short miles north of DeGrasse.

- 47.0 The turnoff to Lampsen Falls is just about 4 miles north of DeGrasse on CR 27. The sign (on the left) says only WILD RIVER, but the locals know it as Lampsen Falls. There are almost always cars parked at the turnoff, mostly students from St. Lawrence University in nearby Canton. From the paved road, it is about a half-mile to the falls along a wide, hard-packed, well-delineated trail—well worth the effort of pushing your bike. There are even primitive campsites scattered about the falls area. I suggest you spend some time here. Lock the bike to a tree and check out the various trails that crisscross the area. After visiting the falls, continue north on CR 27.

- 53.0 Turn right (east) at the intersection of CR 27 and 24 onto CR 24.
- 54.0 Turn right (east) onto Selleck Rd. Be prepared for loose dogs all along Selleck and Orebed Rds. to the intersection with Wilson Rd.
- 59.0 At the T intersection turn left (north) onto Orebed Rd. Get ready for a nice downhill, followed by a rather sedate uphill
- 60.0 Turn right (east) onto Wilson Rd.
- 61.0 At the T intersection turn right (south) onto Cold Brook Rd.
- 66.0 Return to the starting point at the intersection of NY 56 and Cold Brook Rd.

11

Paul Smiths Trio Rambles

This is a perfect set of three starter tours of the Adirondacks, and will undoubtedly be an eye-opener both for novices and experienced riders. The novices will be pleasantly surprised by the tours' overall ease; if done in the recommended clockwise direction, there are barely any hills, and those that are there are gradual climbs. Both novices and advanced riders alike will be amazed at the fantastic scenery, the road conditions, and the region's overall bicycle friendly ambience. The tours also offer a choice of 10-, 20-, or 30-mile loops, ice cream stores, either low-traffic roads or, in the case of NY 3, a wide, paved shoulder, and—most of all—the flattest bicycle terrain in the region. And starting the tour at the campus of Paul Smiths College provides an opportunity to visit the Adirondack Visitor Interpretive Center, which is just 0.6 mile to the north on NY 30. Doing all these tours in a clockwise fashion lets the rider take advantage of a couple of rather substantial downhills, one on NY 3 descending into Vermontville (Tour 1) and the other on NY 86 into Gabriels (Tours 2 and 3).

The Basics

Start: All these tours begin in the front of the Buxton student center on the campus of Paul Smiths College. Well known throughout the Adirondacks and beyond for its hospitality and ecology programs, the college is immediately adjacent to the intersection of NY 30 and 86.

This intersection is exactly 33 miles south of Malone on NY 30. From the east, take NY 86 west from Lake Placid for 21 miles, passing through Saranac Lake. From the west, take NY 3 east for 6 miles to the intersection with NY 30, where you will turn left and continue on NY 30 for 21 miles. At 14 miles past the intersection of NY 3 and 30, NY 30 will take a sharp turn to the left (north). If you miss that turn, you will be on NY 186. (Not a bad place to be, but not where you want to be.)

Length: 10, 22, or 32 miles.

Terrain: If done in a clockwise direction, then 10- and 22-mile loops offer a lightly rolling terrain. On the 32-mile loop, you will encounter a bit of a climb just after you reach NY 3. But the scenery off to you left will more than make up for it.

Food: On the 10-mile loop, there are a couple of small businesses in Gabriels, about 6 miles into the tour. On the 22- and 32-mile loops, the mountain hamlet of Bloomingdale has a general store and a restaurant.

Paul Smiths Ramble 1: Paul Smiths—Gabriels—Paul Smiths

Miles & Directions

- 0.0 From the Paul Smiths campus, go straight across NY 30 onto NY 86, where you will find a wide, paved shoulder.
- 1.0 Turn left onto CR 3 (Jones Pond Rd.). Not much of a shoulder here, but you are not likely to need it since traffic is usually very light.
- 4.0 Turn right onto CR 30 (Gabriels-Onchiota Rd.) and get your camera ready; there will be abundant photo opportunities for the remainder of the tour.
- 6.0 At the hamlet of Gabriels turn right onto NY 86. Note the ice cream store at the intersection of CR 31.
- 10.0 Return to the intersection of NY 30 and 86.

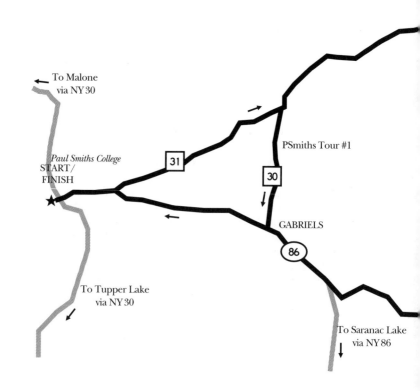

Onchio

To Malone
via NY 30

Paul Smiths College
START/
FINISH

31

PSmiths Tour #1

30

GABRIELS

86

To Tupper Lake
via NY 30

To Saranac Lake
via NY 86

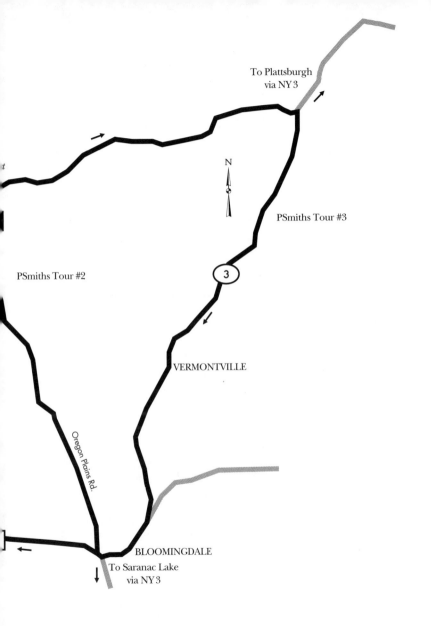

To Plattsburgh
via NY 3

N

PSmiths Tour #3

PSmiths Tour #2

3

VERMONTVILLE

Oregon Plains Rd.

BLOOMINGDALE
To Saranac Lake
via NY 3

Paul Smiths Ramble 2: Paul Smiths—Bloomingdale—Gabriels—Paul Smiths

Miles & Directions

- 0.0 From the Paul Smiths campus, go straight ahead across NY 30 onto NY 86. You will find a wide, paved shoulder at this point.
- 1.0 Turn left onto CR 31. Not much of a shoulder here, but you are not likely to miss it since traffic is usually very light.
- 4.0 Turn left onto CR 30.
- 7.3 Turn right onto Oregon Plains Rd.
- 12.8 Enter the village of Bloomingdale and turn right onto CR 55. *Note:* To stop for a snack or a meal, continue straight in to the center of the village, where you will find the Norman General Store. To continue the tour, backtrack out on the street you came in on (State St.) and bear left onto CR 55.
- 16.6 CR 55 will merge with NY 86. There's a nice paved shoulder from here on all the way back to Paul Smiths.
- 17.8 Hamlet of Gabriels. Both a grocery and an ice cream store are available. Continue straight on NY 86.
- 21.8 Return to Paul Smiths College.

Paul Smiths Ramble 3: Paul Smiths—Onchiota—Vermontville—Bloomingdale—Gabriels—Paul Smiths

Miles & Directions

- 0.0 From the Paul Smiths campus, go straight ahead across NY 30 onto NY 86. You will find a wide, paved shoulder at this point.
- 1.0 Turn left onto CR 31. Not much of a shoulder here, but you are not likely to miss it since traffic is usually very light.

- 4.0 Turn left onto CR 30 and get your camera ready; there will be abundant photo opportunities for the remainder of the tour.
- 8.0 Prepare to stop in the community of Onchiota, where you should take the time for a tour of the Onchiota International Airport (no jets). Continue on CR 30.
- 14.0 Turn right onto NY 3, which offers a fine wide, paved shoulder and more great scenery. Here you will start a gradual climb. After about 0.5 mile, you will come to a rest area on your left. This is a good opportunity to take in some fantastic Adirondack scenery. The biggest peak in the distance is Mt. Marcy to the east, more than 5,000 feet high. Continue on NY 3.
- 18.0 You will commence a long downhill into Vermontville, again with unbelievable views of the Adirondacks all around.
- 19.0 Pass through the hamlet of Vermontville. There is only one opportunity to stop in Vermontville, a small general store/gas station on your right as you zoom down the big hill. If you are not really hungry, you may want to wait about 5 miles until you reach Bloomingdale, where there is a real general store and a few more snack opportunities.
- 24.0 At Norman General Store in Bloomingdale, turn right onto State St. and follow it around to the left where it becomes St. Regis St. and then CR 55.
- 27.0 CR 55 blends into NY 86. Here you again encounter a rather nice paved shoulder. Get ready for a brisk downhill into Gabriels.
- 28.0 Pass through Gabriels. Note the ice cream store on your right as you are leaving the village. After Gabriels, the paved shoulder becomes even wider.
- 32.0 Return to intersecton of NY 86 and 30.

12

Lake Placid Sentinel Range Challenge

Lake Placid—Keene—Upper Jay—Jay—
Wilmington—Lake Placid

For decades, the name of Lake Placid, New York, has evoked images of the Olympic Winter Games, with world-class athletes careening down perfectly groomed ski trails. It used to be that to mention Lake Placid meant snow, but it's no longer just that. During the (albeit short but very pleasant) summer, the snow-covered ski trails are replaced by fantastic summer scenery and a road system that is very bicycle-friendly, particularly along this tour. This tour passes by the Olympic ski installations.

The Basics

Start: At the intersection of NY 73 and 86 in Lake Placid (just a few yards from the most famous bike/outdoor shops in the entire Adirondacks, High Peaks Cyclery, as well as the Lake Placid Olympic Center). If you need anything associated with cycling, skiing, or skating, this is the place.
Length: 41 miles.

Terrain: Moderately hilly to hilly if done in a counterclockwise direction but *very* hilly in a clockwise direction. There is more than 2,000 feet of climbing in 40-plus miles no matter which way you do it. If you are going in the recommended counterclockwise direction (Keene, Upper Jay, Jay, and Wilmington in that order), the initial 7 miles or so will be a gradual climb. From there you will have a 7-mile stretch the length of Cascade Lake and then a roaring downhill into Keene. From Keene to Jay is a rather flat stretch along the Ausable River. At Jay you will start climbing again and will continue to do so all the way back to Lake Placid.

Food: Being an Olympic venue, the immediate area around Lake Placid is loaded with upscale everything—bike shops to clothing stores to restaurants. There are a few restaurants in Keene and a general store in Jay. From there to Wilmington and back to Lake Placid, there are plenty of eateries along the route.

Getting there: (It's a hike no matter how you do it!)

From the Albany area, take I–87 north for about 100 miles and NY 73 for about 43 miles into Lake Placid.

From Plattsburgh, take I–87 south for about 15 miles to NY 3 and then NY 3 for 31 miles to Jay. At Jay, turn right onto NY 86 for another 18 miles or so to Lake Placid.

From the Syracuse area, take I–81 north for 70 miles to Watertown and then NY 3 for 120 miles to Saranac Lake. From Saranac Lake, take NY 86 for 9 miles to Lake Placid.

Miles & Directions

- 0.0 Take NY 73 south toward Keene. Expect some climbing for the first 7 miles or so. Then you may expect a series of downhills all the way into Keene (mile 14).
- 14.0 At Keene, turn left (north) onto NY 9N. This will be a rather flat, sedate stretch and extremely scenic with the

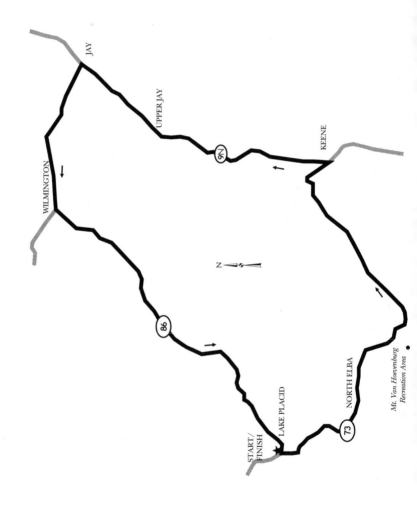

JAY

UPPER JAY

KEENE

9N

WILMINGTON

N

86

Mt. Van Hoevenburg
Recreation Area

LAKE PLACID

NORTH ELBA

START /
FINISH

73

east branch of the Ausable River generally off to your right. At around mile 20 you will pass through the hamlet of Upper Jay.

- 23.5 At Jay be prepared to turn left (west) onto NY 86. In Jay you will find a real general store off to the right as you approach the intersection with NY 86 and the turn to Wilmington. There also used to be a covered bridge in Jay, but the state transportation department replaced it with a modern bridge a few years ago, placing the old bridge on the ground a short distance away from the new bridge. After making the left (west) turn onto NY 86, expect the steepest climb of the day all the way into Wilmington.
- 28.6 At Wilmington, NY 86 turns sharply to the left. At mile 34.1 you will pass through the Wilmington notch, where the road narrows considerably. This could be a bit tight if there are a lot of big trucks or RVs around. But the notch area is less than 300 yards long, and the shoulder picks up again immediately. Nevertheless, remember to exercise extreme caution when passing through the notch.
- 40.6 Return to the starting intersection of Highways 73 and 86.

13

Tour of the St. Lawrence Valley Classic

The tour of the St. Lawrence Valley represents a classic tour of 270-plus miles along both sides of the St. Lawrence River where it forms the border between the U.S. and Canada. For convenience sake, the overall tour has been broken into three segments of about 90 miles each. They include the potential for four international river/border crossings—three breathtakingly huge bridges and one "Toonerville trolley" ferry.

Cycling in the St. Lawrence Valley offers several advantages. For starters, the terrain, with a few minor exceptions, is lightly rolling, certainly manageable by even relatively inexperienced riders. By inexperienced, I mean folks who had never ridden their bicycles more than 25 miles at one time in their lives. They not only make it all the way, they also love doing it. Another advantage of this route is the condition and construction of the roads. On the New York side, NY 37 and 12 offer a wide, paved shoulder from Massena all the way to Cape Vincent with rather light traffic. And the backroad traffic is even lighter. Even the condition of the backroads themselves is, in general, very good. Next, you have beautiful vistas of the St. Lawrence River, which very often include the sight of majestic ocean-going ships coming and going along the seaway. Finally—and this is a purely subjective observation based on several years of cycling throughout the St. Lawrence Valley—the area's drivers have a live-and-let-live attitude toward cyclists. Obviously there are exceptions. But in general, cycling in this region is marked by an acceptance and welcoming of bicycle tourists. Except for the Massena area, northern New York is rather devoid of heavy industry. So tourism reigns, and bicycle touring is becoming a part of it.

The biggest draw of the area lies just across the river: eastern Ontario from Kingston downriver to Cornwall. Cycling is said to be Canada's number one outdoor activity, and I believe it. Canadians take their cycling very seriously, which is reflected in the fact that, in general, Ontario drivers are very courteous toward cyclists. And businesses along the loop welcome touring cyclists by actively promoting bicycle tourism (bicycle maps abound) and accommodating bicycle tourists. The biggest problem with cycling in Canada is the fact that wide, paved shoulders, such as those found in New York, are rather rare. This is changing, however. For instance, within the past year or so, a sufficiently wide paved shoulder has been added to Ontario 2 between Kingston and Gananoque—right where we want to go!

So what's the downside, you might ask, to cycling the St. Lawrence? There are basically two. The first, of course, is its remoteness. It is a fact that the St. Lawrence Valley is sort of off the beaten path; you really have to want to go there. On the other hand, I have often heard visiting cyclists praise that very aspect. The second downer to cycling the St. Lawrence is the wind. It seems that there is always a stiff wind coming downriver from Kingston toward Massena. Some days are worse than others and can be very discouraging to novice riders. On the other hand, when you are struggling upriver, just think about the fantastic run downriver you will have after you finally make your turn. In general, because it is remote, because the roads are so good, because the drivers are nice, and because tourism is the main industry (with reasonable prices), bicycle touring in the St. Lawrence Valley is particularly rewarding—the wind notwithstanding.

So the following classic tour grew out of a genuine appreciation for cycling throughout the St. Lawrence Valley (and the Adirondacks). The first segment is the loop covering Massena, Ogdensburg, Morrisburg, Ontario, and Cornwàll, Ontario.

The second segment covers the area between Ogdensburg and Alexandria Bay, while the third includes the area from Alexandria Bay upriver toward Kingston, Ontario.

Segment 1: Massena to Ogdensburg

Start: Massena, Orvis and Main Sts. This intersection is adjacent to the Flanders Inn (10 W. Orvis St., Massena, NY 13662, 800–654–6212), probably the best motel in the area. It offers reasonable rates and has allowed cyclists riding the St. Lawrence Valley loop to park in its lot.

From the Syracuse area, take I–81 north about 95 miles to NY 12. Take NY 12 northeast for 29 miles to its intersection with NY 37. Continue northeast on NY 37 for 48 miles to Massena. Turn left at the intersection of NY 37 and Main St. Follow it for about one-half mile to the intersection of Main and Orvis. The Flanders Inn will be on your left.

From Albany take I–87 about 180 miles north to the intersection with NY 3 at Plattsburg. Take NY 3 west for one mile and then turn right (north) onto NY 90 for 24 miles to Ellenburg, New York. At Ellenburg, turn left (west) onto US 11 for 20 miles to the intersection with NY 211. Take NY 211 west for 11 miles to its intersection with NY 37. Turn right onto NY 37 for 28 miles to the intersection with NY 37B. Turn right onto 37B (east Orvis) for one mile to its intersection with Main St. From this direction, the Flanders Inn will be on your right.

Length: 97 miles.

Terrain: Lightly rolling. In fact, if one could squeeze another 3 miles or so out of the tour, it would be among the flattest centuries in history. Since it requires crossing two huge bridges, it is not recommended for anyone with a severe case of vertigo.

Food/services: On the U.S. side, the first restaurant will be after about 10 miles. There are several restaurants in Waddington, about 20 miles into the tour, and a general store at Red Mills, almost halfway between Waddington and Ogdensburg. Once across the bridge into Canada, villages and stores are every 3 to 5 miles.

Miles & Directions

- 0.0 Start this tour by going north on Main St. toward the St. Lawrence River. After about 1.3 miles, the name of the street will change to N. Pontoon Bridge Rd. Regardless of the name, continue straight.
- 2.7 At the T intersection turn left onto Hwy. 131. Here you encounter a fine paved shoulder extending all the way to Ogdensburg. On your right will be the St. Lawrence River. After a half-mile you will cross the Massena Intake Dam.
- 4.0 At the stop sign, turn right to remain on 131.
- 10.2 Turn right onto NY 37.
- 20.0 At the blinker light in Waddington (the only traffic light in the village), turn right (north) onto Main St. and continue all the way, about 2 blocks, to the river. *Note:* If you are considering stopping for a picnic at the Waddington town beach on the banks of the St. Lawrence, the center of Waddington offers the only opportunity to buy supplies.
- 20.2 Turn left onto St. Lawrence Ave. and continue for 2.1 miles to the Waddington town beach. With a shelter house, rest rooms, and changing facilities, this is perfect for a picnic stop. To regain the tour route, retrace your path a few yards by going left out of the park to the very first street, Buck Rd. Turn right (south) onto Buck Rd. for about 0.4 mile to regain NY 37.
- 20.6 Turn right (west) onto NY 37. This will take you all the way to the international bridge at Ogdensburg, 14.3 miles away.
- 35.0 Turn right onto NY 812 and the access road to the bridge.

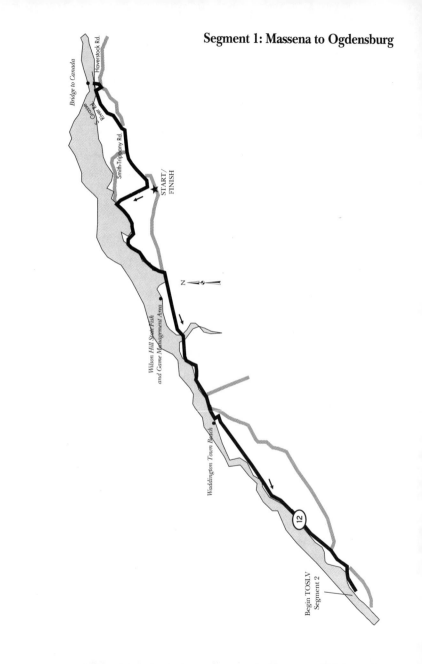

Segment 1: Massena to Ogdensburg

Bridge to Canada

Haverstock Rd.

S. Grasse River Road

Smith-Trippany Rd

START/
FINISH

N

Wilson Hill Sport-Fish
and Game Management Area

Waddington Town Beach

12

Begin TOSLV
Segment 2

Note about crossing the bridge and passing through Canadian Customs: I have crossed the bridge in both directions several times. However, because of the steel grate construction, I have always pushed my bike along the small, 1.4-mile-long walkway on the west (upriver) side. I have also always ignored the NO PEDESTRIANS signs. If you are wearing cleated cycling shoes, remember to pack a pair of walking shoes for the bridge. Finally, you must have a picture ID for Canadian Customs.

- 38.0 After passing through Canadian Customs, continue straight out to the highway, Ontario 16, and turn right (south) for less than half a mile to Ontario 2.
- 38.5 Turn left (east) onto Hwy. 2. After about 5 miles you will pass through the village of Cardinal. Stay on Hwy. 2.
- 47.0 You will come to the village of Iroquois, a fitting stop for a picnic. Look for signs directing you to the St. Lawrence Seaway Lock, off to your right about 1 mile. There you will find a refreshment stand and a park where one can view the ships being lifted or lowered through the lock. Otherwise just continue eastbound on Hwy. 2 for another mile and a half.
- 48.5 Turn right onto CR 4. This is a pleasant, low-traffic road that runs parallel to the river and will eventually bring you back to Hwy. 2.
- 55.0 At the intersection of Ontario 2, be prepared to turn right (east) onto Ontario 2. However, this is an intersection that offers a couple of amenities. To your left is a nice motel (the Loyalist) and to your right a rather nice shopping center with a bakery. I have stayed overnight at this intersection at least twice while leading groups on the full 270-plus-mile loop. However, if stopping here does not fit your plans, cycling an additional half an hour farther east on Ontario 2 will bring you to the area's primary tourist attraction, Upper Canada Village, which has all the amenities of a first-class resort including a very nice restaurant, a golf course, and even an airfield.
- 62.0 Upper Canada Village: At this point, since you are

only about 3 hours by bike from your starting point in Massena, you should seriously consider stopping off for the night and dedicating at least half a day to touring Upper Canada Village. It's one of those total immersion experiences, where the interpreters, local folks all, are dressed in period costumes and everyone has gone to extreme lengths to recreate an 1860s atmosphere, even to the point where some of them have learned the dialect spoken here then. This is a first-class educational experience for kids and grown-ups alike, and very reasonably priced. When you leave Upper Canada Village, continue eastbound on Hyw. 2.

- 64.0 You will encounter a sign to the Upper Canada Migratory Bird Sanctuary off to your right. Take the turn and you can bid good bye to Hwy. 2 forever, for you will soon be on a system of very pleasant nature trails, parkways, and multi-use trails all the way into Cornwall. For example, the 7-mile Long Sault (pronounced Sue) Parkway crosses no fewer than eleven islands. The western end is connected directly to the Upper Canada Migratory Bird Sanctuary trail and the other end to the Cornwall Bike Path. The distance between the bird sanctuary and the Cornwall Civic Center is 21 miles. However, about 1 mile before the civic center, this tour will leave the trail to get onto the Cornwall International Bridge, which will bring you back into the United States.

- 84.0 Immediately after passing under the big bridge, turn left and follow the bridge to the traffic circle. Go all the way around the circle and get onto the bridge proper. Immediately after coming off the bridge, you will come to a toll booth. Make sure you go around the booth. (Bikes are free.) Next you will go around the Canadian Customs building and then keep cycling onto the second bridge. Though both bridges look rather narrow and dangerous from afar, when you get onto them, you will discover that there is sufficient room for bikes and cars to co-exist.

- 88.0 Shortly after coming down off the second bridge and

passing through U.S. Customs, you will come to another traffic circle exactly 3 miles from the traffic circle on the Canadian side. Take the first exit off the circle onto CR 45 for 0.25 mile.

- 88.3 Turn right onto Haverstock Rd. for almost 3 miles.
- 91.2 Turn right onto S. Grasse River Rd. for less than 1.5 miles.
- 92.6 Turn right onto Smith-Trippany Rd. for a bit over 1 mile to O'Neil Rd.
- 93.6 Turn left onto O'Neil Rd. for just a few yards and then right onto NY 37 for 2 miles to the turnoff onto 37B into Massena proper.
- 95.6 Turn right onto 37B for about 1.5 miles to the center of the village.
- 97.1 Return to your starting point at Orvis and Main Sts.

Segment 2: Ogdensburg—Alexandria Bay

The instructions for finding the starting point of this segment are pretty much the same as for segment 1. From the Syracuse area, the directions are the same to the intersection of NY 12 and 37. Ogdensburg is only 12 miles beyond the intersection of NY 12 and 37. Once in Ogdensburg, take NY 812 north (becomes State St.) for 1 mile to the Remington Museum on your right.

From the Albany area the same instructions apply to Massena. At Massena just continue southwest on NY 37 for another 38 miles to Ogdensburg. Once in Ogdensburg, take NY 812 north to the Remington Museum on your right.

Start: The Frederic Remington Museum in Ogdensburg at State and Washington Sts.

Length: 91 miles.

Terrain: This loop is just a bit more rolling than segment 1, but there are no killer hills.

Food/Services: There is no shortage of good restaurants along this tour. Even tiny Waddington has a very nice deli.

The best restaurants,, however, are in Alexandria Bay and Brockville, Ontario. The best German deli in southeast Ontario is the Prescott Deli on Main Street in Prescott.

The only full service bike shops on this loop are in Brockville, Ontario: Dave Jones Sports (for sales and repairs, 65 King Street West, K6V 3P8 (613) 345–5574), QJ Johnny (for sales and repairs, 198 King Street West, K6V 3R5 (613) 342–5543), and the Racer's Edge Pro Shop (for repairs only, 6 Dehli Street, K6V 4H3 (613) 345–2133).

Miles & Directions

(The starting point for this segment is 2.82 miles from where segment 1 turns onto the Cornwall International Bridge. If you are continuing directly onto segment 2 from segment 1, your total mileage at the start of segment 2 will be 37.82 miles. For simplicity's sake, segment 2 begins at 0.0 miles.)

- 0.0 From the front of the Remington Museum, go west on Washington St., which will soon become the downtown arterial. Follow it around, keeping straight ahead to cross the river, and in just a few yards you will cross the bridge over the Oswegatchie River. While crossing the bridge, glance to your right toward the St. Lawrence River and note the point of land on the left bank of the Oswegatchie where French Jesuits built a mission called La Presentacion in the early 1750s. Promptly attacked and burned by British settlers, the mission was rebuilt by the French and called Fort La Presentacion. In 1753, some Indians from the fort journeyed south to participate in the French victory over General Braddock just outside Pittsburgh.
- 0.5 As you come down off the bridge, turn left onto New York Ave. and continue for 0.9 mile to NY 37.
- 1.4 Continue straight across NY 37. At that point, New York Ave. becomes Black Lake Rd. or CR 6.
- 2.2 Turn right (west) onto Monkey Hill Rd. for 2.6 miles to a T intersection with Lee Rd.
- 4.8 Turn right (north) onto Lee Rd. for 0.5 mile.

Segment 2: Ogdensburg—Alexandria Bay

- 5.3 Turn left (west) onto Haggert Rd. for 6.1 miles. Note that Haggert Rd. becomes Center Rd. after crossing Scotch Bush Rd.
- 11.4 Turn right (north) onto English Settlement Rd. for 1.8 miles to NY 37.
- 13.2 Turn left (west) onto NY 37 for 0.4 mile.
- 13.6 Turn right (northwest) onto Champlain St. for 0.6 mile to Main St. in Morristown.
- 14.2 Turn left onto Main St. for 0.2 mile to Northumberland Rd.
- 14.4 Turn right onto Northumberland Rd., which soon becomes River Rd. for about 2.4 miles to a dead-end and turn left onto Old Mills Rd. for about 0.4 mile to NY 12.
- 17.2 Turn right (west) onto NY 12 and prepare yourself for over 26 miles of river vistas—and not much else. Indeed, the next civilization will be 10 miles away, at the turnoff into the river hamlet of Chippewa Bay. By the time you get to Chippewa Bay, you will be ready for a short break at the small general store right on the river bank. And since the road (CR 93) loops back out onto NY 12, you will not lose very much time. Barely 2.5 miles west of Chippewa Bay is the turnoff to Schermerhorn Landing, where a little restaurant sells great milkshakes. But no matter what, keep going west on NY 12.
- 38.5 You will pass Church St., the main access road into Alexandria Bay, on your right. This is far and away the biggest tourist area in the St. Lawrence Valley and worth an extended stop, maybe even an overnight stay. Resort and motel accommodations can run the gamut from insanely expensive ($100-200 per night) to very reasonable ($40-50 per night). There is also camping at Kewadin State Park just a couple of miles west of Alexandria Bay on NY 12. Keep on truckin' westbound on NY 12 for another 4 miles or so and get ready to cross the Thousand Islands International Bridge.
- 44.2 You will cross under the approach to the bridge. Just 0.3 mile farther, turn right (north) at the CITGO station

(the first road after the bridge) for about 100 yards and turn right (east) again onto Collins Landing Rd. for another 0.5 mile and follow the signs to the Thousand Islands Welcome Center, located right at the end of the big bridge.

- 45.0 Though no formal signs tell you what to do, the steel grating of the bridge's road surface will: Walk your bike the 1.3 miles across the bridge along the narrow sidewalk on the upriver (west) side. For this you will need regular walking or touring shoes.

- 46.3 After crossing the bridge, take the first turn off to the right for just a few yards and turn left (north) onto CR 191 for 3 miles where you must get back onto I–81 just in time to go through Canadian Customs.

- 50.0 Pass through Canadian Customs and into Canada. The road has now shrunk down to two rather busy lanes. After about 0.5 mile, you will encounter a second bridge across the St. Lawrence which, as with the previous bridge, you must walk across on the upriver (west) side. Though not as big as the first one, it definitely has an adventurous aspect to it, especially since there is no barrier or railing between the teeny-weeny sidewalk and the adjacent roadway. And pushing a heavily laden touring bike along a narrow sidewalk, across a windy bridge, with cars and trucks passing within inches, can be quite an adventure, particularly toward the north end where you will encounter a gap of less than 3 feet through which you must maneuver. Anyone with a severe case of vertigo would do well to think twice before walking this particular bridge.

- 52.0 After successfully navigating across the second bridge, continue straight for just a few 100 yards and and turn right onto Ontario 2. Then, almost immediately, cross over both lanes of traffic to gain the Thousand Islands Bike Path, easily visible on the north side of the road.

Note: Between Gananoque and the western outskirts of Brockville, you will be cycling along the Thousand Islands Bike Path, a dedi-

cated multi-use trail 8 feet wide and about 21 miles long.

- 63.0 Upon reaching the end of the Thousand Islands Bike Path, continue straight across the roadway, jog left and then right onto Butternut Rd. for about 2 miles before rejoining Ontario 2. A rather big motel at that intersection, Alexander's, has a full-service restaurant.
- 65.0 Turn right (east) onto Ontario 2 for 7 miles into Brockville, where you will encounter many nice restaurants.
- 72.0 Brockville. Stay on Ontario 2 through Brockville. There will be a nice paved shoulder from Brockville to Maitland.
- 74.0 Turn left (north) onto the Maitland Rd. for about 1 mile to the Second Concession Rd.
- 75.0 Turn right (east) onto the Second Concession Rd. for 7 miles to CR 18.
- 82.0 At the T intersection of Second Concession Rd. and CR 18, turn right (south) onto CR 18 for 1 mile to the intersection with Ontario 2.
- 83.0 At the intersection of CR 18 and Ontario 2, you will be turning to the left (east) for about 3 miles to the Ogdensburg Bridge. You will be in Prescott, which though small, has an ice cream store and a great German delicatessen (the Prescott Deli), which will be on your right-hand side if you turn right (westbound) onto Ontario 2 for less than a block.
- 86.0 You will pass under the Ogdensburg/Johnstown Bridge. If you intend to stop cycling after completing this segment, you must cross this bridge and return to Ogdensburg.
- 86.4 Turn left (west) onto the bridge access road. From here it is less than 2 miles across the bridge to U.S. Customs.
- 88.0 Turn right onto Proctor St., the first real street to the right after departing U.S. Customs.
- 88.9 Turn right onto Ford St. for just over a half mile.
- 89.5 Turn right (north) onto Roseel St. until it ends at Washington St.

- 89.6 Turn left (west) onto Washington St.
- 90.5 Arrive at your starting point in front of the Remington Museum.

Segment 3: Kingston Loop Classic

Start: Thousand Islands Welcome Center at I–81 and NY 12.
Length: 70 miles.
Terrain: Mostly lightly rolling on the U.S. side. On the Canadian side, a bit hillier for the 20 miles between Kingston and Gananoque. The biggest hill of the entire loop is just east of Kingston, where Ontario 2 climbs up the hill by Fort Henry.
Food/Services: Since this segment of the tour passes through three major vacation destinations—Kingston and Gananoque, Ontario and Alexandria Bay, New York—the number of excellent restaurants increases expotentially over segment #2. There are too many to list here.

There are also at least three full service bike shops in Kingston. On the U.S. side, the bike shop nearest the route is Ray Kimball's Professional Bicycle Service (315–649–2929), which is about 14 miles from Cape Vincent on the Point Salubrius Road near Chaumont, New York.
Getting there: From Syracuse, take I–81 northbound for about 93 miles to the NY 12 southbound exit. On NY 12, turn immediately to your right at the CITGO station onto Seaway Ave. for 0.1 mile. Take the first turn to the right, Collins Landing Rd., for about 0.4 mile and you will be at the Thousand Islands Tourism Council Center (800–8ISLAND).

From Albany, go west on I–90 for about 93 miles to exit 31. Go west on I–790 for about 1.5 miles to NY 5. Go east on NY 5 for just 0.2 mile to NY 49. Go west on NY 49 for 16 miles to NY 69. Go west on NY 69 for 17 miles to Camden. Go north on NY 13 for 25 miles to I–81. Go north on I–81 for 56 miles to NY 12 westbound (exit 50). This will take you onto NY 12 west. After passing under the Interstate, take the first road to your right,

Segment 3: Kingston Loop Classic

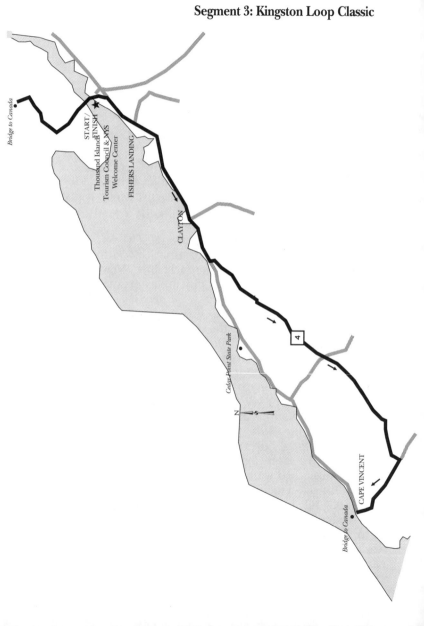

Bridge to Canada

START / FINISH
Thousand Island
Tourism Council & NYS
Welcome Center

FISHERS LANDING

CLAYTON

Cedar Point State Park

N

4

CAPE VINCENT

Bridge to Canada

Seaway Ave. There is also a CITGO gas station on this corner. After turning onto Seaway, take the first turn to the right onto Collins Landing Rd. and continue to where it ends in the parking lot of the Thousand Islands Tourism Council Center.

Miles & Directions

- 0.0 From the Thousand Islands Tourism Council Center parking lot, take the exit road out to Seaway Ave.
- 0.4 Turn left (south) onto Seaway Ave. for 0.1 mile.
- 0.5 Turn right (west) onto NY 12 for 6.8 miles to the first light in Clayton.
- 7.3 Continue straight onto 12E for 2 miles to CR 4.
- 9.3 Turn left (southwest) into CR 4 for 12.5 miles to NY 12E.
- 21.8 Turn right (north) onto NY 12E for 3.1 miles to Point St. Here you should see signs to the ferry. Turn left into Point St.
- 22.0 Arrive at the Cape Vincent ferry station. In 1998, the fee for rider and bicycle was $1.00, either Canadian or U.S. currency.
- 22.0 Depart Canadian Customs on Wolfe Island and proceed across the island on the only paved road (CR 95). After 7 miles, turn right at the T intersection onto CR 96 for about 0.3 mile and then left down the hill to the ferry landing.
- 30.0 Upon leaving the ferry at the Kingston dock, turn right at the first intersection onto Ontario 2. You will soon cross a steel grate bridge and then have the opportunity to climb the biggest hill of the tour. Remain on Ontario 2.
- 50.0 Arrive in Gananoque.
- 52.0 At the east end of Gananoque, take the right-hand exit onto the Thousand Islands Parkway. Only after getting up onto the parkway will the paved bike/pedestrian path be easily visible to the left.
- 62.0 When the bike/pedestrian path ends, you must get

out onto the parkway itself for a very short segment. *Note:* If you are continuing on the Canadian side, the bike path picks up again just a few hundred yards farther east. It is very easy to see. Otherwise follow the signs for the BRIDGE TO THE USA. The bridge is also free for cyclists and pedestrians and can be a bit exciting, since there is no railing between the roadway and the raised sidewalk (at least on the Canadian side). If the wind is blustery, it might be necessary to hang onto the railing to prevent being blown onto the roadway. You will cross two huge bridges—a Canadian and then an American one. Getting through U.S. Customs can sometimes be unpleasant since there is no special lane for pedestrians or cyclists and you must wait in line with the cars.

After passing through U.S. Customs, take the small exit road off to the right down to the first crossroad. Turn left and cross under I–81 and then turn right at the T intersection onto CR 191. Continue on for 4 miles to the T intersection and turn right onto CR 100. As you come under the big bridge, you must leave the roadway and push your bike through the grass and come up onto the bridge. With a stout railing between you and the passing cars, this bridge is a bit less scary to cross, in spite of the fact that the sidewalk is rather narrow. Coming off the bridge, the Thousand Island Tourism Council Visitor Center and New York State Welcome Center is easily visible to the right.

Note: If you are continuing on the Canadian side, pick up the instructions at mile 52 from segment 2.

Saranac Lake Duo

The following two tours are centered on the Adirondack community of Saranac Lake, which is less than 15 miles from its famous Olympic neighbor, Lake Placid. Saranac Lake also lies at the junction of two important and bicycle friendly highways, NY 3 and 86, both of which offer fine paved shoulders. With skiing in the winter and everything else in the summer, the Saranac Lake area offers a myriad of year-round recreational opportunities without the hectic atmosphere of Lake Placid. For cyclists, this means not only road touring but mountain biking, too. Road touring is facilitated by the fact that the other main area highways, 9N and 73, also offer paved shoulders. Even the backroads, while not equipped with shoulders, have plenty to offer with great scenery and very little traffic. For mountain bikers there are literally miles and miles of trails and unpaved backroads. In regard to cyclists in general, there seems to be a live-and-let-live attitude among area drivers, both local and tourists alike—probably because just about everybody who comes into this area has either a road or a mountain bike strapped to the back of his or her car or RV. So bicycles are everywhere throughout the Adirondacks, on the main roads as well as the backroads. This is also reflected in the presence of very good bike shops in both Lake Placid (including the famous High Peak's Cyclery) and in Saranac Lake (Barkeater Bicycles at 49 Main Street). Both the Saranac Lake tours use the same starting point, which makes separate morning and afternoon tours possible and simplifies parking.

Both of these tours will take you along Forest Home Road. This is a great road for either a short day trip or getting into

Saranac Lake from Malone to the north or Tupper Lake to the west. It's scenic and shady and has a low traffic volume. However, it is home to a few loose dogs, so when cycling Forest Home Road, or in general along the backroads of the Adirondacks, always take some protection against dogs.

The Basics

Start: On the north edge of Saranac Lake at Ampersand Rd. and NY 86; there is plenty of parking all around this intersection. From Malone, take NY 30 south for about 33 miles to NY 86. Paul Smiths College, the starting point for the three Paul Smiths tours, is located at this intersection. Turn left onto NY 86 for 12 miles all the way into Saranac Lake. The start location, Ampersand Road and NY 86, is the first traffic light in Saranac Lake. From Lake Placid, take NY 86 west toward Saranac Lake and stay on it all the way through Saranac Lake (about 9 miles). The intersection you want is the last one in Saranac Lake with a traffic light. From Tupper Lake, take NY 3 east for about 20 miles into Saranac Lake and follow the signs for NY 86 through Saranac Lake to the last traffic light in town.

Saranac Lake Tour 1: Paul Smiths Loop Cruise
Saranac Lake—Paul Smiths College—Gabriels—Donnelly's Soft Ice Cream—Saranac Lake

Length: 30 miles.
Terrain: Definitely hilly, but the hills are not major. The longest climb will be outbound on Forest Home Rd. for about 6 miles. In addition to the normal ups and downs, there is another noticeable climb when departing Gabriels (about mile 23) on NY 86. Except for Forest Home Rd., you will have a paved shoulder for the entire trip.
Food: At the intersection of NY 30 and 186, about 10 miles into the tour, is a small refreshment stand with pleasant outside seating. There is also a snack bar at the Paul Smiths campus about 17 miles into the route. Four miles beyond Paul

Smiths, the hamlet of Gabriels has an ice cream store and a grocery on your left. The best ice cream stop of the day is, without a doubt, Donnelly's Soft Ice Cream Shop at the intersection of NY 86 and 186, about 25 miles into the tour. For real gourmet dining, try the Hotel Saranac, the headquarters for the Paul Smiths College Hospitality Program, which continually produces world class chefs!

Miles & Directions

- 0.0 Cycle west onto Ampersand Rd., which will curve around into a southerly direction.
- 0.7 Turn right (west) onto Forest Home Rd., also known as CR 18. The initial 6-plus-mile stretch will have its ups and downs, mostly ups, before leveling out somewhat beyond McMaster Rd. When it does level out on top, be prepared for loose dogs.
- 8.0 At the end of Forest Home Rd., turn right (northeast) onto NY 30.
- 10.0 At NY 186, turn left to remain on NY 30. For a snack, continue straight on 186 for a few yards to the Kilroy's Corner refreshment stand. Afterward, return to the intersection and continue north on 30 toward Paul Smiths College. Off to your left will be some rather nice views of Lake Clear.
- 17.0 At the intersection of NY 30 and 86, turn right onto 86. However, before making this turn, plan on a short stop at Paul Smiths College, which will be on your left. Named after a pre–Civil War hotelier who ended up owning vast tracts of Adirondack woods, Paul Smiths College is one of the few institutions of higher learning in the Adirondacks. Specializing in ecology and the hospitality industry, it produces great environmentalists and even greater chefs. The college welcomes visitors to both its main campus and its hospitality program headquarters at the Hotel Saranac in Saranac Lake. If you care to make this stopover even more

Osgood Pond

86

Paul Smiths College

Spitfire
Lake

Upper Saint
Regis Lake

30

N

Donnelly's
Ice Cream Factory
& Store

Lake Clear

LAKE CLEAR

86

Lake Colby

STAR
FINISH
★

18

Forest Home Rd.

fruitful, continue north on NY 30 for about 0.6 mile to the Adirondack Visitor Interpretive Center, which will provide you with vast amounts of information on the area and even offers guided tours and nature trails. This is well worth the stop and can turn this half-day ride into an all day educational adventure.

When you are done at Paul Smiths and/or the information center, continue east on 86. The wide, paved shoulder continues all the way back to Saranac Lake.

- 21.0 Pass through the hamlet of Gabriels. There will be at least one ice cream store and a grocery on your left. Leaving Gabriels you will encounter a 1-mile climb, not overly steep but definitely an uphill pull and worthy of any granny gear.
- 25.0 Pass through the intersection of NY 86 and 186—and go no farther, for you have arrived at Donnelly's Soft Ice Cream Shop, a must-do for any passing cyclist! Delicious ice cream is made right there on the premises. This is not Baskin-Robbins with 31 flavors, but you will have no regrets. When finished at Donnelly's, just continue in the same direction on NY 86 for about 5 miles into Saranac Lake.
- 30.0 Arrive back at the starting point of Ampersand Rd. and NY 86.

Saranac Lake Tour 2: Fish Creek Pond Ramble
Saranac Lake—Fish Creek Pond—Saranac Lake Inn—Forest Home Road—Saranac Lake

Length: 36 miles.
Terrain: This is definitely the hillier of the two Saranac Lake tours, particularly between Saranac Lake and NY 30. However, the condition of the road and the fine paved shoulder (not to mention the fantastic scenery) should more than make up for

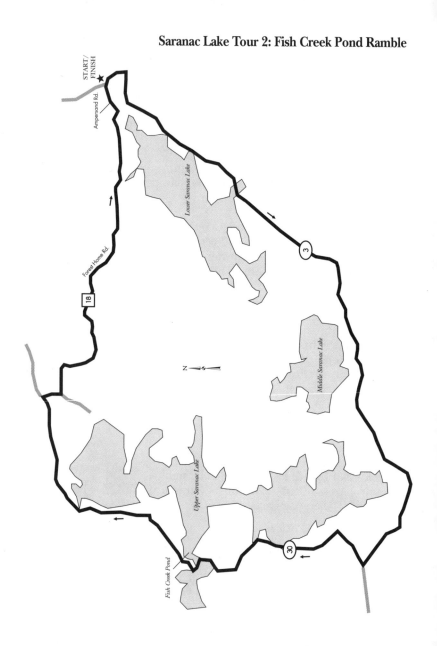

Saranac Lake Tour 2: Fish Creek Pond Ramble

START/
FINISH

Ampersand Rd.

Lower Saranac Lake

3

Forest Home Rd.

18

Middle Saranac Lake

N

Upper Saranac Lake

30

Fish Creek Pond

the exertion. Once you start north on NY 30, the road levels out quite a bit. Shortly after making the final turn onto Forest Home Rd., you will (no ifs, ands, or buts) enjoy the 4-mile downhill.

Food: Rather sparse until you reach the Fish Creek Pond area (mile 20.2), where there is a general store on your right that caters to campers from the state park. Because of the exertion of climbing the hills along NY 3, take plenty of water.

Miles & Directions

- 0.0 Go west on Ampersand Rd. for 0.8 mile to Edgewood Rd.
- 0.8 Turn left onto Edgewood Rd.
- 1.0 Turn right onto NY 3. Get ready for some hill-climbing for the next 14 miles or so.
- 15.3 Turn right onto NY 30.
- 20.2 Pass the Fish Creek Pond General Store on your right.
- 24.1 Turn right onto CR 46.
- 25.1 Turn right onto NY 30.
- 27.2 Turn right onto Forest Home Rd. (CR 18).
- 34.8 Turn left onto Ampersand Rd.
- 35.5 Arrive at starting point.

Adirondack Gran
Tour Classic

Thendara—Croghan—Cranberry Lake—
Long Lake—Thendara

This circular tour goes from the light rollers between Port Leiden and Lowville to the real Adirondack hills, which begin near Harrisville and continue all the way around to Old Forge. While it is a great touring route, the Adirondacks can be quite a challenge and are not for the faint of heart. The good news is that, except for the 14-mile stretch along Moose River Road, you should encounter a paved shoulder for most of this 196-mile tour. That's right—paved shoulders most of the way, with great scenery, and scores of B&Bs and restaurants. The only item lacking in this scenario is an abundance of bike shops. While Utica has plenty of bike shops, the only ones you will encounter on this route are World Cup Ski, Board, and Bike (69 Park Street, Tupper Lake, NY 12986, 518–359–9481) and Pedals & Petals (176N, Rte. 28, P.O. Box 390, Inlet, NY 13360, 315–357–3281) is exactly what the title says, a floral/gift shop in front with a full-service bike shop in the rear. While most of the Pedal & Petals business is in mountain bikes (there are miles and miles of great mountain bike trails in the area), the Adventure Cycling Northeast Extension to Bar Harbor, Maine, goes literally right by the front door! But whatever is lacking in numbers of bike shops is

---

more than made up for in scenery, particularly north of Croghan. More—much more—about Croghan later.

So what more could you want from a four-day tour: fantastic scenery, cozy B&Bs, great food, safe shoulders for most of the 200-mile ride? How about a *railroad*? In fact, how about *two railroads*? First, you can ride AMTRAK, and check your bicycle (packed in a box, of course) to Utica. But once in Utica, that's where the fun begins. Since August 1998, the Adirondack Scenic Railroad (ASRR) has run twice-daily service between Utica and Thendara, just outside Old Forge. If you want, you can even dump your AMTRAK box in Utica and roll your bike on and off the ASRR train as in Holland. The convenience and reasonably priced fares make this tour a possibility for cyclists without a car or those purists who want to avoid using a car to travel to a bicycle tour.

The ASRR line ends in Thendara. Less than a mile from Old Forge and the railroad station, there is a great place to begin the tour, particularly since one of the best hotels in the Adirondacks, Van Auken's Inne, is right across the street, not 60 feet away.

The Basics

Start: Adirondack Scenic Railroad station in Thendara.
Getting there (by car): From Utica, take NY 12 north for 24 miles to Alder Creek. Turn right (northeast) onto NY 28 for 23 miles. The railroad station will be on your right.

From Albany, take I–90 west for 96 miles to Utica. Then follow the directions above.

From Lake Placide, take NY 86 west for 10 miles to Saranac Lake. From Saranac Lake, take NY 3 west for 21 miles to Tupper Lake. From Tupper Lake, take NY 30 south for 30 miles to Blue Mountain Lake. From Blue Mountain Lake, take NY 28 west for 36 miles to Old Forge. Continue on 28 through Old Forge for 2 miles to Thendara. The railroad station will be on your left.

Length: 196 miles.
Terrain: Light rollers the first day, major hills from then on.
Food/services: Since the Adirondacks are rather sparsely populated, you will not find a fast-food restaurant around every bend. As a matter of fact, sometimes you might have to cycle 10 to 20 miles to find anything except forests and streams. But good food, friendly folks, big chain motels and resorts, campgrounds and countless cozy B&Bs abound in the communities all along this route. Since this is a prime vacation area, it is a good idea, particularly during the summer, to make reservations through the local Chambers of Commerce. On the Internet, check www.digitalchambers.com.

Miles & Directions

Day 1: Thendara to Croghan

Length: 50 miles.
Terrain: Light rollers.

- 0.0 When you leave the railroad station, turn right for a few yards, cross the tracks, and voilà, you will be at the intersection with NY 28, the actual starting point of this tour. Turn left (west). You will have a fine paved shoulder for 9 miles to the Moose River Rd. turnoff.
- 9.0 Immediately after crossing the Moose River, turn right (northwest) onto Moose River Rd., a small, shady country lane with beautiful vistas and picnic sites right next to the Moose River for about the first 5 miles. After 5 miles, the shade and vistas remain but the road pulls away from the river, so enjoy your waterside picnic while you can.
- 19.0 You will come to a fork in the road with no signs. Moose River Rd. goes straight ahead toward Port Leiden, while the left-hand side of the fork takes you to Boonville, a lovely little village in its own right but slightly out of the way.

CROGHAN

N

Adirondack
Museum

118

★
START/
FINISH
THENDARA

- 22.0 Moose River Rd. ends at a T intersection with a rather substantial cemetery crossing the T. Turn right (north) onto River Rd. for just a few hundred feet to CR 39.
- 22.1 Turn left (west) onto CR 39 for less than a mile.
- 23.0 Turn right (north) onto NY 12. This is a rather busy road, but you will now have a wide, paved shoulder all the way to Inlet.
- 38.5 As you enter Lowville from the south, you will encounter a couple of rather nice restaurants. Country Bob's is on the right (it also has a rather inexpensive motel) and Lloyds of Lowville on your left, right at the intersection of NY 12 and 26. Continue straight ahead on 12 into and through Lowville proper.
- 39.5 Turn right (east) onto NY 812. *Note:* Right at that intersection of 812, 12, & 26, there is a very nice B&B, the Victoria House.
- 50.0 Croghan. This little village is recommended for the first overnight stop on this tour. With a predominantly Mennonite population, the village is squeaky clean and the people very friendly. However, it is small. On a bike you could probably see everything there is to see in 30 minutes. In addition, Croghan also has great ice cream *and* chocolate stores, one of each. For ice cream, it's Good Ole Wishy's, right in the middle of the village on Main St. You can sit at the old fashioned ice cream counter and watch the cones, sodas, and shakes being mixed by hand. And just a few hundred feet farther along, on the other side of the street, is a great confectionary, the Croghan Candy Kitchen. Finally, you might want to try some of the famous Croghan bologna, available in the local markets.

Day 2: Croghan to Cranberry Lake

Length: 52 miles.
Terrain: Hilly.

- 50.0 Leave Croghan going north on NY 812.
- 56.0 Pass through Indian River. At this point, the route becomes progressively hillier.
- 66.5 Turn right (east) onto NY 3, the Olympic Hwy.
- 69.8 Pass through the village of Harrisville.
- 70.8 NY 812 bears left. Continue straight on NY 3.
- 73.0 Pass through the hamlet of Pitcairn, the last civilization for about 15 miles.
- 87.5 Turn left onto CR 60 (Newton Falls Rd.). There are a couple of rather serious uphills between here and Newton Falls, not long but definitely an uphill pull. However, they are child's play compared with the 3-mile climb you just avoided on NY 3 going into Star Lake.
- 91.8 In the hamlet of Newton Falls, replenish water bottles at the Newton Falls Hotel, the biggest show in town. Then turn left (east) onto River Rd.
- 98.0 At the T intersection with Tooley Pond Rd., turn right (south).
- 100.7 Turn left (east) onto NY 3.
- 101.7 Pass through the hamlet of Cranberry Lake. The Cranberry Lake Inn, located on your right on the lakefront has rooms and a restaurant.

Day 3: Cranberry Lake to Long Lake

Length: 47 miles.
Terrain: Hilly.

- 101.7 Continue eastbound on NY 3.
- 110.0 Pass intersection of NY 3 and 56. Remain eastbound on NY 3. FLASH! A new convenience store has recently opened at this intersection, Ham's Mini Mart, open seven days a week. The next real restaurant will be Dumas's in Childwold (mile 113).
- 113.0 Pass through the hamlet of Childwold. Dumas's restaurant, on your right, will be your last chance to re-

plenish water bottles or buy snacks until you reach the outskirts of Tupper Lake about 15 miles away.

- 127.0 Pass through the village of Tupper Lake. Turn right (southwest) onto NY 30, a scenic, relatively flat road (at least until the Hamilton County line) with a wide, paved shoulder and plenty of picnic stops along the way. *Note:* The next civilization is in Long Lake, about 24 miles away. Make sure you replenish water bottles and snacks prior to departing the Tupper Lake area.
- 149.0 Village of Long Lake. A recommended stopover for the night is the Adirondack Hotel on your right. Enjoy watching the seaplanes take off and land directly across the road from the hotel.

Day 4: Long Lake to Thendara

Length: 48 miles.
Terrain: Hilly.

- 149.0 Continue south on NY 30. At the T intersection of 28N/30, turn right onto 28N. The route will become even more hilly from this point on. The great Adirondack scenery and the fine wide, paved shoulder, however, should help ease some of the hardships of hill-climbing.
- 156.7 You will see a sign for Blue Mountain Lake as well as a steep grade warning. At this point, you are almost at the Adirondack Museum—in fact, you are almost on top of it! When you pass over the crest of the hill and start down the other side, keep your brakes on for a mere 0.3 mile to the museum entrance.
- 157.0 The Adirondack Museum, one of the top regional museums in the nation, will be on your right. Your biggest problem will *not* be finding it (the very large parking lot and prominent signs make that easy) but slowing down enough to turn into the lot. If you miss the turnoff, it's a

rather stiff climb back up the hill. So take it easy—if you can—going down that big hill.

- 159.0 Bear right (west) onto NY 28. The paved shoulder narrows quite a bit along here but remains usable. Remember, you are on the Adventure Cycling Northeast Extension to Bar Harbor, Maine, and it will not be unusual to meet long-distance riders from here all the way to Thendara.
- 183.4 Turn left onto CR 1. *Note:* If you need a bike shop, continue on 28 for less than a mile to Inlet, where you will find the Petals & Pedals bike/florist shop on your left. When you are done in Inlet, you must backtrack to CR 1, now on your right. CR 1, Lake Shore Rd., becomes CR 118 and then becomes CR 54.
- 194.4 Bear left onto Park St. In less than 0.5 mile, Park St. becomes Railroad St.
- 195.0 Turn right (north) onto Joy Tract Rd. for about 0.1 mile to rejoin NY 28.
- 196.0 Where NY 28 bears right, remain straight on Forge St. for a few hundred yards and you will come back to your starting point, the ASRR station on your right.
- 196.3 Thendara railroad station.

Congratulations!

Suggested equipment for an Adirondack tour:

- Complete tool kit, including chain tool and extra links, chain lube, extra tube and tire, and extra brake cables (which can easily double as shifter cables)
- Two big water bottles (three if you have room)
- If you are camping, *an extra long rope* to hang up your food between two trees. The bears and raccoons in the Adirondacks are incredibly adept at figuring out how to relieve campers of food supplies. However, because of the shortness of this tour, I suggest you forget about camping and stay in motels and B&Bs. They are all quite reasonable in price. During the day, you will have no problem finding

gorgeous picnic sites. If you do decide to camp, there are numerous campgrounds along the route.

- *Strong insect repellent* for the pesky black flies and mosquitoes.
- Some sort of deterrent for loose dogs, like a can of pepper spray.
- Rain and/or cool weather gear. Winter stays longer and comes earlier with a vengeance to these parts. Take a cell phone if you have one.

New Jersey

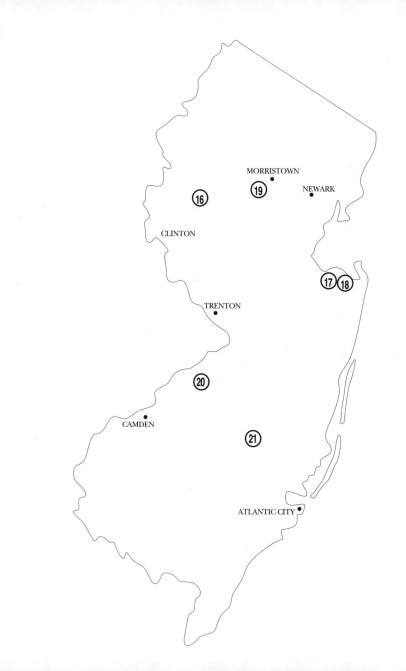

MORRISTOWN
•

⑲

NEWARK
•

⑯

CLINTON

⑰⑱

TRENTON
•

⑳

CAMDEN
•

㉑

ATLANTIC CITY
•

New Jersey

Raritan River Gorge Ramble

Clinton—Califon—Clinton

This peaceful meander in western New Jersey is one of the nicest you're likely to encounter. In late June, the route is festooned with wild rose, fragrant honeysuckle, and edible mulberries. It is so shaded that it would be cooling on even a hot day. With very little traffic, gently rolling terrain, the scenery, particularly the Raritan River gorge, is unparalleled. So slow down; bring your fishing rod, binoculars, and picnic lunch, and introduce a friend to the joys of bicycle touring. Based on a route contributed by Leonard C. Friedman and Gail Waimon of Short Hills, New Jersey, and verified by Donald R. O'Rourke, this charming tour starts in the town of Clinton in Hunterdon County. There you can park either along the street or in the public lot in back of the Clinton Bakery, where you can pick up breakfast, snacks, or lunch on any day but Monday. Clinton's small historic downtown district is worth a walking tour, particularly the Hunterdon Historical Museum (908–735–4101) and Hunterdon Art Center (908–735–8415), two former gristmills on either side of the cast-iron bridge that carries Main Street over the river. The Clinton Falls Country Store and Eatery overlooking the waterfall is a nice place to relax for a drink or bowl of soup after the ride. Clinton does not have any bed-and-breakfasts, but the Holiday

---

Inn is at 111 Route 173 (908–735–5111).

You'll leave Clinton by Center Street, which is lined by mature gingko and maple trees and gracious old homes. The ride from Clinton to Califon, which follows the Raritan River upriver, is a net uphill. But it is generally very gentle, with the few notable inclines short enough only to make you glow.

The highlight is the 1.8-mile unpaved section of Raritan River Road (uniformly abbreviated RIVER RD. on the street signs), which parallels the fast-flowing, boulder-strewn south fork of the Raritan River deep in the rocky wooded gorge of Ken Lockwood Gorge Park. Although the well-maintained gravel and dirt road can be navigated even by thin-tire bikes, you will be happier on a hybrid or true mountain bike, especially if you come back on the Columbia Trail. In any event take your time, maybe even pause for an hour or two to watch the birders gazing through their spotting scopes or the fly fishermen in waders casting for rainbow, brown, and brook trout.

Your destination, Califon, feels like the town that time forgot. The roads are so sleepy that geese sit right in the middle of them, hammocks swing from front porches, and the nineteenth-century buildings of the bank and general store still have false fronts (170 of these structures are included on the National Register of Historic Places). Sit by the river to enjoy your picnic lunch.

Should you wish to revisit the river gorge and have a generally easy return, just retrace your outbound route. You will find several restaurant and grocery stores in Califon, mainly around the intersection of Routes 512 and 513. Another choice is to take the Columbia Trail, which requires a .1 mile trip up the hill west from the Califon Post Office on Route 512. You turn right onto the trail just past the Califon Historic Society railroad station, which is open from 1:00 to 3:00 P.M. on the first and third Sunday from May through September. The trail itself is the old railroad bed and is now home to a Columbia Gas Company pipeline. Part of the Hunterdon Park System and signed as such, the trail is passable on a thin-tired bike but is maintained only about half as well as the dirt section of Raritan River Road. It ends at Route 513 in High Bridge.

The Basics

Start: Take I–78 to exit 15, following Rte. 173 (Hunterdon County Rte. 513) to Clinton. Turn right at the traffic light by the Clinton Municipal Building, which is an old white mansion. This is Leigh St. Go past Main St., which is one-way the wrong way, turn left onto Center St. and left again into the large parking lot behind the bakery.
Length: 18 miles.
Terrain: Flat to gently rolling; if you return on the Columbia Trail, a few hills on Rte. 513.
Food: Available in Clinton and Califon.

Miles & Directions

- 0.0 Turn right out of the public parking lot onto Center St. Set your odometer to 0.0 as you pass through the first intersection with Leigh St. on one side and Halstead St. on the other.
- 0.7 Left at the traffic light for Rte. 31N.
- 0.9 Left at the T intersection with a traffic light still heading for 31N. Now you're pedaling on an entrance ramp for 31N.
- 1.0 Right on Grayrock Rd. just before the onramp joins 31N. Grayrock Rd. immediately becomes a country lane passing through cornfields.
- 2.1 Right onto Jericho Rd. at a T intersection with a stop sign. Soon the river will parallel your path on the left.
- 2.9 Right at the T intersection. Continue on Arch St. and

ride through the right arch of the double-arched stone underpass, paralleling the river, which flows through the left arch.

- 3.3 Right at the T intersection with a stop sign. Continue on Washington Ave.
- 3.5 Bear left to stay on Washington Ave.
- 3.7 Bear left again to stay on Washington Ave.
- 3.9 Go straight over a babbling brook. Now you are on Rte. 639 (River Rd.).
- 4.9 Left at the stop sign by the dark green house, no. 450, and a quick right to stay on River Rd.
- 5.5 Paved road surface ends.
- 7.1 Surface returns to pavement.
- 7.4 Cross Hoffmans Crossing Rd. and continue straight on River Rd.
- 9.1 Right onto Rte. 612 at the stop sign opposite the Califon Post Office.
- 9.2 Right at the Califon Historic Society and Columbia Trail. To take the trail for your return, you will have to maneuver your bike across two bridges, each with two locked gates. However, the gates have sufficiently wide openings to let hikers and cyclists pass through.
- Return mileage via the Columbia Trail (recommended).
- 10.7 Cross Hoffmans Crossing Rd. straight onto the trail.
- 11.6 Cross the bridge over the Raritan River.
- 14.2 Left at Rte. 513 in High Bridge.
- 14.7 Left at Arch St. and a quick right onto Jericho Rd. This is the same way you left Clinton.
- 15.5 Left on Grayrock Rd. at a T intersection with a stop sign.
- 16.6 Left just before Rte. 31 stop sign.
- 16.7 Right at traffic light to cross over Rte. 31 for Clinton.
- 16.9 Right at traffic light on Center St.
- 17.6 You are back where you started at Leigh and Halstead Sts. The bakery is to your left. Enjoy!

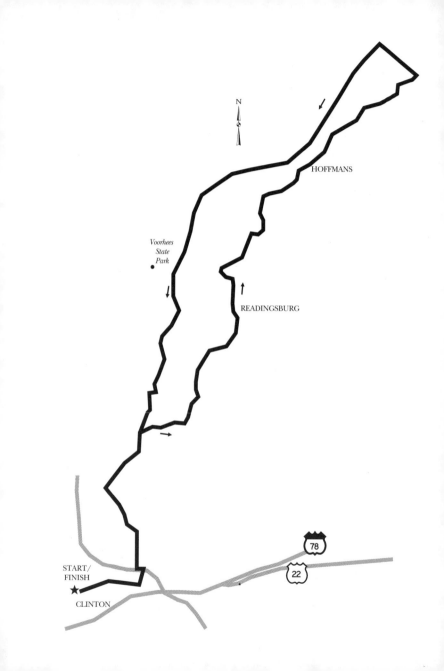

N

Voorhees State Park

HOFFMANS

READINGSBURG

78

22

START/
FINISH

CLINTON

Return mileage on the road.

- 9.2 Left coming out of the Califon Historic Society Museum onto Rte. 512.
- 9.3 Left on Rte. 512 to cross the river on a white bridge.
- 9.9 Left onto Rte. 513 at the traffic light with the food stores.
- 12.1 Cross Rte. 528. Stay straight on Rte. 513.
- 12.7 Pass Voorhees State Park and Voorhees High School.
- 14.5 Right on Church St. to stay on Rte. 513.
- 14.6 Left on Main St. to stay on Rte. 513. You cross the end of the Columbia Trail as you turn.
- 14.7 Right on Rte. 513 under the NJ Transit High Bridge station.
- 15.1 Left at Arch St. and a quick right onto Jericho Rd.
- 15.9 Left at Grayrock Rd. at a T intersection with a stop sign.
- 17.0 Left just before Rte. 31 stop sign.
- 17.1 Right at the traffic light to cross over Rte. 31 for Clinton.
- 17.3 Right at the traffic light on Center St.
- 18.0 You are back where you started at the intersection with Leigh and Halstead Sts. The bakery is to your left. Enjoy!

Holmdel Park and the Spy House Ramble

Parkway exit 120—Holmdel Park—The Spy House—Exit 120

The following two tours both begin at the commuter parking lot at exit 120 of the Garden State Parkway. They can be done in a morning and afternoon without having to move your vehicle from one starting point to another. One can also get to within 2 miles of this starting location via non-rush-hour NJ Transit trains. For information on transporting your bike, call NJ Transit at (201) 491–9400. Train information is available on its Web site: www.njtransit.state.nj.us/.

When you leave the Matawan train station, go north 1.8 miles on Aberdeen Road, the only road parallel to the tracks, to the commuter parking lot. You can also take your bike on the Academy Bus Line to Hazlet. When you get off the bus at Route 36 and Middle Road, go left (north) on Middle Road one half-mile to Maple Place. Turn left (west) on Maple Place and go 0.3 miles to Broadway and pick up the trip at mile 16.2 by turning right at the traffic light with two convenience stores. Academy may be contacted by calling (212) 971–9054, (212) 962–1122, or (732) 291–1300.

The Basics

Start: The commuter parking lot at exit 120 of the Garden State Parkway. This is immediately adjacent to Cheesequake State Park. While there is access from the lot to the mountain bike trails in the state park, the rangers prefer that everyone enter via the main entrance. To get into the state park, motorists must pay $5.00 per car on weekdays and $7.00 per car on weekends from Memorial Day to Labor Day, but cyclists are admitted free. Once inside you can swim in the lake or hike or bike the trail system. Camping is available at $10.00 a night with a two-night minimum plus a $7.00 registration fee. Reservations are necessary only in the summer. The phone number is (732) 566–2161.

Length: 32 miles.

Terrain: According to verifier Rory O'Rourke, this tour has a few hills with generally good visibility. Furthermore, he urges caution when crossing Rte. 34 at mile 9.2, where there is a curve in one direction and a hill in the other, making it somewhat difficult to judge the heavy traffic.

Food: The best selection of stores on the trip is at the first intersection of Laurence Pkwy. and Morristown Rd. at mile 0.2. For about 5 miles after leaving there, you will encounter a surprising amount of farmland. Beacon Hill Rd. is fully tree-shaded and has a gentle upgrade with views of lower Manhattan in the winter. After that you will never be very far from convenience stores. However, it is always prudent to pack along a minimum of emergency snacks such as Fig Newtons or gorp.

Homdel Park, at mile 10.4, a day park with chickens, sheep, goats, pigs, and lots of ducks that is very popular with family groups. There is no admission charge to this Monmouth County Park, which also offers extensive hiking trails through fields and woods. Local schools hold cross-country races there on Saturdays.

Beginning around mile 12, Briar Hill Rd. takes you through the Fox Hill subdivision with its million-dollar homes. It is scenic and pleasant if you don't mind the continuous din of traffic from the nearby Garden State Parkway.

Around mile 20, you will encounter the major historical feature of this tour. The Holmes-Henderson House, with its fine view of Sandy Hook Bay, was built before the American Revolution. According to local legend, the Holmes were loyalists and spied for the British during the Revolution. Thus, the house is known in these parts as "the spy house," and is administered by the Middletown Historic Society. It is surprising that the house has lasted so long since the area is prone to flooding during winter storms from the northeast.

Around mile 21, you will have the opportunity to ride a 5-mile segment of the Henry Hudson Trail, a former railroad bed now paved over. Thirteen miles long, the trail crosses many bridges over tidal water and offers opportunities to catch crabs. It ends in Keyport, an important industrial center during World War I, when all U.S. Navy seaplanes were built there. Industry left Keyport long ago, replaced by numerous genteel antiques shops and marinas. You will also see many yachts when you cross Matawan Creek. Keyport is also home to Steamboat Dock Musuem (732–739–3140), right by the water on American Legion Dr.

Miles & Directions

- 0.0 From the commuter parking lot at exit 120 of the Garden State Parkway, turn right onto Matawan–Laurence Harbor Rd. and then, 0.2 mile later, make another right at the large Exxon station onto Morristown Rd.
- 0.5 Bear left at the traffic light for Gordon Rd. to stay on Morristown Rd.
- 0.9 Turn left onto Disbrow Rd. Watch for oncoming traffic.
- 1.2 Cross Rte. 34 to remain on Disbrow Rd.
- 1.6 At the stop sign turn left onto Amboy-Freneu Rd.

Holmes-
Henderson
House

Henry Hudson Trail

N

Garden State Parkway

Holmdel
Park

START/
FINISH
Exit 120

- 2.2 Turn right onto Morganville Rd.
- 2.4 Cross Rte. 516. Shortly thereafter, Morganville Rd. becomes Greenwood Rd.
- 3.6 Cross Ticetown Rd. to remain on Greenwood Rd.
- 4.6 At the stop sign turn left onto Tennant Rd., then right onto Church Rd. and right again onto Rte. 79 at mile 4.9.
- 5.3 Turn left onto Beacon Hill Rd.
- 7.1 At the stop sign turn right onto Reids Hill Rd.
- 7.6 Bear slightly left where Reids Hill Rd. becomes Pleasant Valley Rd.
- 8.4 Turn left onto Schanck Rd.
- 9.2 Cross Rte. 34 using extreme caution. The terrain makes oncoming traffic difficult to see.
- 9.6 At the T intersection turn right onto Rte. 4 (Holmdel Rd.).
- 9.8 Turn left onto Roberts Rd., which becomes Longstreet Rd.
- 10.4 The entrance to Holmdel Park will be on your left. This is a nice rest stop with rest rooms. Upon leaving the park, turn left to continue on Longstreet.
- 11.5 At the T intersection turn right onto Crawfords Corner–Everett Rd. Shortly thereafter, turn left onto Holland Rd.
- 12.4 Turn right onto Briar Hill Rd. Get ready for views of some million-dollar homes. Take the first left onto Rosewood and then turn left again for a very short stretch on Telegraph Hill Rd. and right onto Huntley Rd., which will turn to the right and go downhill. At the bottom of the hill (mile 13.2), turn left onto Cross Run Rd.
- 13.5 Turn left onto Galloping Hill, which will turn to the right and then left. At mile 13.6 turn left onto Fox Hunt Rd. and follow it around to where you will encounter a T intersection with Van Schoick Rd. where you turn left at mile 13.8.
- 14.6 Turn right onto Holland Rd.
- 15.7 At the stop sign turn left onto Red Hill Rd.

- 15.9 Turn left onto Kings Hwy.
- 16.5 Cross Rte. 35. Kings Hwy. becomes Harmony Rd.
- 17.2 Turn right onto Rte. 516 (Cherry Tree Farm Rd.).
- 17.8 Turn left onto Wilson Ave.
- 18.8 Cross Rte. 36. There is a deli at this corner. Remain on Wilson Ave. all the way to the water.
- 19.8 At the T intersection turn left onto Port Monmouth Rd. Here you will find the Holmes Hendrickson House and the Green Acres Fishing Pier with public rest rooms on your right.
- 20.9 Turn left onto Bray Ave.
- 21.2 Turn right onto Thompson Ave.
- 21.6 Just before crossing Rte. 36, turn right onto the Henry Hudson Trail. You will be on this trail for about 5 miles.
- 26.1 In Keyport bear right onto Maple Pl. This intersection is unsigned, but the Cornucupia Restaurant is across the street.
- 26.2 Turn right at Broad St. There will be a 7-Eleven store at the intersection.
- 26.6 Bear left by the boat launch on American Legion Dr. and continue to the water.
- 27.0 Bear right onto W. Front St., which becomes Amboy Rd.
- 27.7 Turn right onto Prospect Ave., which becomes Woodmere, which, in turn, becomes Sunset Dr.
- 28.9 Turn right onto Beachwood Way. (You just went in a circle around the point.)
- 29.0 Turn left onto North Concourse.
- 29.4 Turn left onto Greenwood Ave.
- 29.5 Bear right onto Cliffwood Rd.
- 29.9 Cross Rte. 35. There is a McDonald's at this intersection.
- 31.4 After crossing over the Garden State Parkway, turn right onto Matawan–Laurence Harbor Rd.
- 31.6 Turn left into the commuter parking lot.

Parkway Exit 120 to Jamesburg Ramble

Start: This is the second of two tours that begin at the commuter parking lot at exit 120 on the Garden State Parkway. This tour is flatter than the Holmdel Park tour and offers an opportunity to visit Mendoker's Bakery. (More about that later.) The western, or Jamesburg, terminus of this tour is at Middlesex County's Thompson Park, which features a lake, a petting zoo, large fields, large trees, picnic tables, and a popular spring.

Length: 38 miles.

Terrain: According to tour contributor Rory O'Rourke, this tour is much flatter than the preceeding Holmdel tour. In addition, the scenery is about one-half new residential development and the other half mostly orginal woods and farm fields. In Spotswood you will pass through the most northern part of the Pine Barrens. Finally, the views of the bay and yacht basins in historic Keyport are quite picturesque.

Miles & Directions

- 0.0 Turn right out of the commuter parking lot onto Matawan–Laurence Harbor Rd.
- 0.2 Turn right at the traffic light by the large Exxon station onto Morristown Rd.
- 0.5 Bear left at the traffic light for Gordon Rd. to stay on Morristown Rd.

- 0.9 Turn left onto Disbow Rd. Be careful of oncoming traffic.
- 1.2 Cross Rte. 34 at the traffic light.
- 1.6 At the T intersection turn left onto Amboy Rd.
- 2.2 Turn right onto Morganville Rd.
- 2.4 Cross Rte. 516 at traffic light.
- 3.6 Turn right onto Ticetown Rd.
- 5.6 Turn left onto Stratford St. at a hilltop curve and then right again onto Morningside Dr.
- 5.9 Turn left onto Normal Ln.
- 6.0 Turn left onto Oakland St.
- 6.4 Turn right onto Inverness St.
- 6.6 Turn right onto Rte. 9N.
- 6.9 In order to go in the desired southbound direction on Rte 9, it will be necessary to turn right (north) onto Rte 9 for just a few yards and right again at the first right-hand turnoff. This will swing around to your left and you will be at the traffic light at Cindy Ln. and Rte 9. Turn left (south) onto Rte 9.
- 7.2 Turn right onto Ferry St.
- 7.4 Turn left onto Old Amboy Rd.
- 8.1 At the T intersection turn right onto Spring Valley Rd.
- 8.5 Turn right onto Rte. 18N. This is a merge onto a four-lane road. Get ready for a left turn.
- 8.7 Turn left onto Marlboro Rd.
- 9.1 Turn right onto Pleasant Valley Rd. for a bit of country riding.
- 10.9 At the T intersection turn right onto Rte. 527.
- 11.2 Turn left onto Greystone Rd. Watch for oncoming traffic.
- 12.9 Turn left onto Wilson Ave.
- 13.3 Turn right onto Maple St.
- 13.4 At the stop sign cross Devoe Ave. and continue straight onto Lettau Dr.
- 13.5 Bear left onto Lettau Dr.
- 13.7 At the T intersection turn right onto Erikson, which becomes Spotswood.

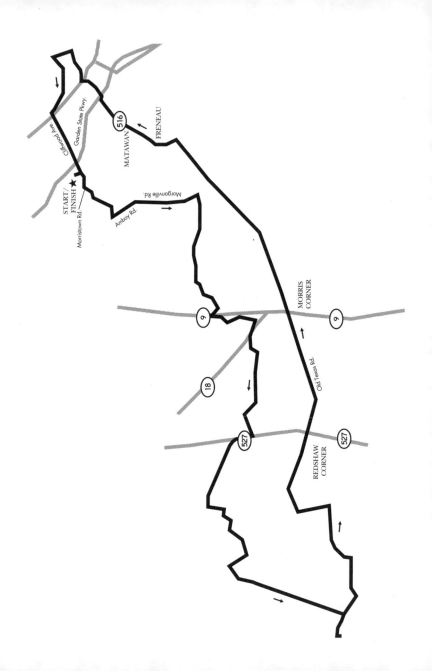

- 14.1 Turn right onto Ellingham Ave.
- 14.5 Turn right onto Tenth St., which becomes Daniel.
- 15.0 At the T intersection turn left onto Rte. 615.
- 15.3 Turn left onto Old Forge Rd.
- 17.5 Turn right onto Pergola Ave.
- 18.0 At the T intersection jog right onto Rte. 612 and then left across the railroad tracks into Thompson Park. Mendoker's Bakery is a half-block from the park on the same side of the railroad tracks.

For the return trip, it is suggested you reset your odometer to 0.0.

- 0.0 Turn right out of Thompson Park onto Rte. 612 the same way you came in. Turn right at the light to remain on Rte. 522 with a view of the lake.
- 0.9 Turn left onto Grace Hill Rd.
- 1.8 At the T intersection turn left onto Spotswood–Gravel Hill Rd.
- 2.1 Turn right onto North State Home Rd.
- 3.1 At the T intersection turn left onto Rte. 613.
- 3.8 Turn right onto Old Texas Rd.
- 5.6 Cross Rte. 527 to remain on Rte. 520 (Old Texas Rd.).
- 8.3 Cross Rte. 9 at traffic light.
- 9.9 Cross Spring Valley Rd. to remain on Texas Rd.
- 11.6 Cross Greenwood Rd.
- 12.6 At the yield sign bear right onto Wilson Ave.
- 12.8 At the T intersection turn left onto Rte. 79.
- 13.1 Cross Rte. 516 at traffic light to remain on Rte. 79.
- 13.4 Cross Rte. 34 at traffic light and go straight on Main St., Matawan, through the center of this charming nineteenth-century town.
- 15.4 Turn left at traffic light for Keyport.
- 15.5 Straight onto Rte. 516 (Maple Pl.) at traffic light.
- 16.6 Turn left onto American Legion Dr. by the bay. The Steamboat Dock Museum (which is open only occasionally) will be on your left. At the T intersection turn right onto W. Front St. The Cottage Inn, a large restaurant with

water views from the dining room, is at this intersection.

- 17.9 Turn right at the Rte. 35 exit followed by a quick left onto Cliffwood Ave.
- 18.0 Cross Rte. 35 to remain on Cliffwood Ave.
- 19.5 Turn right onto Matawan–Laurence Harbor Rd. at the large Exxon station.
- 19.8 Turn left into the commuter parking lot. Watch for oncoming traffic.

19

Great Swamp and Jockey Hollow Cruise

Convent Station—Green Village—Meyersville—
Jockey Hollow—Convent Station

Tours in and around the 6,800-acre Great Swamp National Wildlife Refuge and the Jockey Hollow Encampment Area of the Morristown National Historic Park are ever-popular among nature-loving bicyclists. Even in winter you'll get a wave and a smile from one or two lone riders, and on summer weekends you're likely to be overtaken by a whole group from the Bicycle Touring Club of North Jersey or even from Brooks Country Cycling and Hiking.

The Loantaka Brook Reservation–Great Swamp portion of this ride ranges from flat to gently rolling, with about 1.5 miles of gravel. But the 10-mile extension to Jockey Hollow and the excursion around the park (and any detour to Lewis Morris Park) are very hilly indeed. That is why the full 30-mile ride is designated a cruise. The 20-mile option, which by-passes Jockey Hollow, is a nice early-season ramble even for an out-of-shape novice.

When you are first pedaling through the forest and farm-land, watching sheep graze in the meadows and turtles swimming in the swamp, you'll hardly believe that the grubby, noisy canyons of New York City are only 25 miles away. As in all wildlife areas, you will see more animals in the spring and fall, especially at dawn or dusk. Pack a small pair of binoculars and tiptoe out on the wooden boardwalks to the bird blinds to watch great blue herons majestically standing in the marsh or swallows swooping for insects. Take along hiking boots and spend an hour or two midway through the ride exploring some of the marked but undeveloped trails. Listen, and in the late afternoon and early evening you will hear a chorus of peepers and frogs. Adjoining the Great Swamp to the east is the 425-acre Lord Stirling Park, home of the Somerset County Environmental Education Center, offering another 8 miles of trails.

As for Jockey Hollow: Despite the myriad out-of-the-way places trying to attract tourists by advertising "George Washington slept here," this is one place where Washington really did sleep, along with 10,000 soldiers. In the winter of 1779–80, they nearly froze and starved in the sheltered hollows of Jockey Hollow during one of the most bitter winters of the Revolutionary War. There are many sites here preserved from those days, as well as historical restorations and minitours by guides in period costume, so take your time wandering through this park after you pay the $4.00 user fee. The park is open daily from 8:00 A.M. to 7:00 P.M.; for more information, call (973) 543–4030. You'll also get a good aerobic workout on its rollercoaster hills.

Adjoining Jockey Hollow is the 1,154-acre Lewis Morris Park (973) 326–7604, on the Web at www.parks.morris.nj.us, a county park where you can pitch a tent for overnight camping. You might also want to pack a swimsuit for a dip in its Sunrise Lake; the sole disadvantage to refreshing yourself in the lake is that, after you're completely clean and relaxed, you must return through Morristown on Routes 24 and 124 because the road back to Jockey Hollow is one-way the wrong way. Because these are wildlife areas, services are few and far between. There are rest rooms and water for your water bottles at Loantaka Brook Reservation, at the parking lot for the wildlife observation area in the swamp, and at the visitor center at Jockey Hollow. There are only two delis near the swamp. On a Sunday you may want to play it safe and pack a lunch, as the Green Village Deli near the start of the ride closes at 3:00 P.M. and The Food Express in Meyersville has limited hours. There are picnic tables and public barbecue grills at Loantaka Brook Reservation and at Lewis Morris Park, but eating within either Jockey Hollow or the Great Swamp is discouraged. Near the end of the ride, though, you can stuff yourself with the blackberries growing alongside the road, ripe in late July.

The Basics

Start: Convent Station, in the Loantaka Brook Reservation at the parking area off Kitchell Rd. To get there, take local Rte. 24, also called Main St., to Convent Station and, just opposite the western edge of Fairleigh Dickinson University, turn south (the only way you can go) onto Kitchell Rd. One mile later turn right to enter the reservation. Here there are rest rooms, water, picnic tables, wooden playground equipment, and a lovely duck pond.
Length: 20.3 or 30.3 miles. Traffic is generally light, with some roads, especially those to Jockey Hollow, a bit more heavily traveled.
Terrain: Flat to gently rolling in the portion touring the Great Swamp, very hilly in the 10-mile stretch to Jockey Hollow.
Food: Only two places to buy snacks or lunch: Green Village Deli 3.7 miles into the ride (closes 3:00 P.M. Sunday) and The Food Express 0.9 mile off the route 9.5 miles into the ride.

Miles & Directions

- 0.0 Start at the northern entrance to the Loantaka Brook Reservation parking lot. Ride straight across narrow

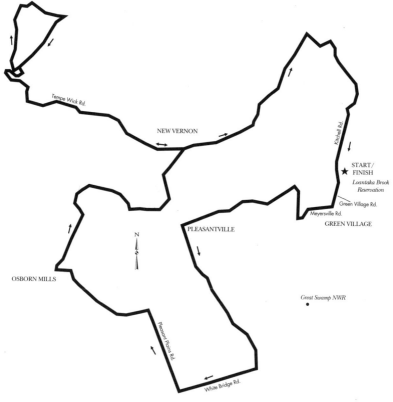

Tempe Wick Rd.

NEW VERNON

Kitchell Rd.

★ START/
FINISH

*Loantaka Brook
Reservation*

Green Village Rd.

Meyersville Rd.

GREEN VILLAGE

PLEASANTVILLE

N

OSBORN MILLS

Great Swamp NWR
●

Pleasant Plains Rd.

White Bridge Rd.

PLEASANT PLAINS

Kitchell Rd. onto the paved bike path, a lovely meander next to Loantaka Brook through forest glades.

- 1.0 Turn right onto the intersecting paved bike path, and follow it as it bends left. At mile 1.5 cross the moderately busy Loantaka Way and continue straight on the paved bike path.

- 2.9 Turn right at the end of the path onto Green Village Rd. Watch for traffic.

- 3.7 Turn left onto Meyersville Rd. (Just before this turn on your right are a Sunoco gas station and the Green Village Deli, the first of the two chances on this ride to pick up snacks or lunch.) Now you're riding through pastoral farmland.

- 4.0 Take the first right (at the NO OUTLET sign) onto Woodland Rd. (Bird-watchers and hikers take note: If you continue straight here instead, in 1 mile the road will end in a small parking area, which is the trail head for some of the nature trails into the northern unmanaged section of the Great Swamp.)

- 4.6 Take the first right (at the NO OUTLET sign) onto Miller Rd.

- 5.1 Turn left at the T intersection onto Pleasantville Rd.

- 6.8 Turn left at the T intersection onto Long Hill Rd. At mile 8.3 is the Wildlife Observation Area gravel parking lot on your right, where you can visit the boardwalks and bird blinds (and rest rooms) at the swamp. To resume the ride turn right out of the parking lot to continue on Long Hill Rd. (which eventually changes its name to New Vernon Rd.).

- 9.5 Turn right onto White Bridge Rd. (*Note:* For the second and last chance to buy snacks or lunch, continue straight through this intersection instead. In 0.9 mile, at the T intersection with Meyersville Rd., is The Food Express. This crossroads is the town of Meyersville. Either the Mexican restaurant Casa Maya or the more formal Meyersville Inn are well worth a dinner stop at the end of the day. Then retrace your route 0.9 mile to this intersection and turn left onto White Bridge Rd.)

- 10.7 Turn right onto Pleasant Plains Rd. to ride into the swamp itself. (*Note:* If you want to visit the Somerset County Environmental Education Center, continue straight ahead on White Bridge Rd. for another 1.3 miles and turn right just after the metal bridge. To continue the ride from there, retrace your route and turn left onto Pleasant Plains Rd. into the swamp.) At mile 11.0 on your right is the Great Swamp National Wildlife Refuge headquarters, which is open Monday through Friday from 8:00 A.M. to 4:30 P.M. and has public rest rooms. Just past the swamp headquarters, the road turns to gravel for the next mile, so ride carefully, following the road as it bends left. A third of a mile later, a gate blocks a bridge to traffic. But the gate is designed to admit pedestrians and bicycles, even those with a child seat on the back. After you cross this bridge over Great Brook, the road is paved once again.
- 13.6 Turn right at the T intersection onto Lee's Hill Rd. Watch for traffic.
- 13.8 Bear left at the fork onto the quiet Baileys Mill Rd., and begin a gentle climb. Up to now the ride has been generally flat; now it becomes gently rolling.
- 14.8 Bear right onto Youngs Rd.
- 15.7 Turn right at the T intersection onto Lee's Hill Rd., and then make an immediate left onto Lindsley Rd.
- 16.4 Turn left at the T intersection onto Long Hill Rd.
- 16.8 Turn right at the T intersection onto Lee's Hill Rd.
- 17.2 Turn left at the traffic light onto Glen Alpin Rd. toward Jockey Hollow. For the shorter 20.3-mile ride, do not turn left; instead pedal straight through this light (at this intersection Lee's Hill Rd. changes its name to Blue Mill Rd.), and pick up the directions at mile 27.2. This is where you'll start doing some serious climbing. At mile 18.9 you'll pass over I-287.
- 19.0 At the light at Rte. 202 (Mt. Kemble Ave.), keep head-

ing straight and uphill onto Tempe Wick Rd.

- 20.4 Turn right at the entrance to Morristown National Historic Park. Keep pedaling uphill.
- 20.8 Just past the visitor center's parking lot, turn right to follow the one-way Tour Rd. (Cemetery Rd.) through the park. (The visitor center has literature, a short film about the park's history, and public rest rooms.) This road now becomes almost a roller coaster, and you may find yourself screaming downhill faster than the posted speed limit of 20 mph.
- 22.1 Bear right onto Grand Parade Rd. at the parking lot for the soldiers' huts, which you can see up on the hill ahead of you. (If you wish to picnic or swim at the adjoining Lewis Morris County Park, a detour that will add a hilly, 2-mile round-trip to your total, turn left instead and coast down to Sunrise Lake. Then return to this point to continue the main ride.)
- 22.6 Turn right at the yield sign to follow the one-way Jockey Hollow Rd. back to the visitor center. At this intersection is a cylindrical building with public rest rooms and a map of the park.
- 23.7 At the visitor center turn left at the stop sign onto the two-way road toward the park exit.
- 24.0 Turn left at the T intersection onto Tempe Wick Rd.
- 25.4 Cross Rte. 202 (Mt. Kemble Ave.) at the traffic light and continue straight onto Glen Alpin Rd.
- 27.2 Turn left at the traffic light onto Blue Mill Rd. At mile 27.3 on your left is Bayne Park, where you can relax on benches and watch geese and ducks in the pond and stream. This manicured park has no facilities or services, not even so much as a garbage can; if you open a snack here, take the remains with you when you leave.
- 28.2 Turn left onto Van Beuren Rd. where Blue Mill Rd. bends right.
- 29.8 Turn right at the T intersection onto Spring Valley Rd. Watch for traffic. In July ripe blackberries dot the bushes

on your right.

- 30.1 Turn left onto Kitchell Rd., braking carefully on the descent.
- 30.3 Turn left into the Loantaka Brook Reservation parking lot.

Smithville Ramble

Mount Holly—Birmingham—Buddtown
Vincentown—Mount Holly

For an easy ride with little traffic through the bucolic beauty of fields, farms, woods, and small towns of historical note, this exploration of Burlington County in southern New Jersey fills the bill. Devised and verified by Rory O'Rourke of Aberdeen, New Jersey, this lovely route is within the abilities of even the most casual cyclist.

After leaving Mount Holly, you'll pedal through Smithville, once the home of the H. B. Smith Works, which made the Star bicycle, famous in the 1890s for its small front wheel and large rear wheel (just the opposite of the traditional pennyfarthing). Smithville is also where the bicycle railway, a treadle-type railroad, was built to carry commuting riders from Mount Holly to the factory at Smithville. On your ride take a moment to stroll through the Smithville Mansion, former home of H. B. Smith; in the summer the mansion's Victorian courtyard is abloom with the profuse, multicolored plantings of a century past.

As you ride through sleepy Birmingham, you'll find it hard to believe that this town was the site of a large tourist hotel in the 1890s, catering to the wealthy of northern New Jersey who escaped to "seclusion in the fresh, aromatic, and healthful air of the pinelands," according to a local history book. Today, however, there are no remnants left.

About two-thirds of the way through the route, a perfect lunch stop is Mill Dam Park in Vincentown, where you can gaze out at a pretty dam and pond. According to O'Rourke, the Riviera Pizza Parlor on Vincentown's Main Street is the only place to eat.

At the end of the ride, when you return to Mount Holly, there are additional places to eat as you go through the center of town and pass both Iron Works Park and Mill Dam Park.

The Basics

Start: In Mount Holly from the Fairground Plaza Shopping Center at the intersection of High and Ridgley Sts. To get to the start, take exit 5 from the New Jersey Turnpike and turn south onto Burlington–Mt. Holly Rd. (Route 541 at this point). Continue straight on this road for 2.3 miles and the Fairground Plaza Shopping Center will be on your left. Park behind either Acme Foods or the Trenton Savings & Loan.
Length: 24 miles.
Terrain: Mostly flat.
Food: Convenience and grocery stores, some restaurants.

Miles & Directions

- 0.0 From the front of the Acme supermarket and Staples, head left, south, on Rte. 691 (High St.).
- 0.8 Turn left onto Rte. 537 (Washington St.) at the second traffic light.
- 1.2 Right on Rte. 621 (Mill St.), which becomes Powell Rd. If you still want a snack, you have your choice of the WaWa Market or the 7-Eleven along the way.
- 3.2 Turn right onto Smithville-Jacksonville Rd. Shortly you will pass the Smithville Mansion on your right. If it is not hosting a wedding reception or other function, take a moment to stroll through the blooming courtyard, refill your

water bottles at the water fountain, or use the public rest rooms off the side entrance.

- 4.0 Turn left onto E. Railroad Ave. just before the railroad bed. (The tracks have been removed.) Now you're riding alongside the railroad bed, which is to your right. Follow the road as it bends sharply left at the end.
- 4.8 Turn right onto Rte. 206, and then make a quick left to cross the busy highway onto Skoneses Rd. You are now in the tiny burg of Ewanville. In 1 block turn right at the T intersection onto Mandas Trail. In another block turn left at the T intersection onto Birmingham Rd. at the INDIAN TRAIL sign. At mile 5.4 cross the railroad bed by bearing right.
- 6.2 At the post office in Birmingham, turn right onto Birmingham-Buddtown Rd. In 0.5 mile watch for traffic while crossing busy Rte. 38 and continue straight.
- 8.3 Turn left at the T intersection onto Pemberton Rd.
- 9.1 Turn right onto Burr's Mill Rd.
- 9.7 Just after the road bends right, turn left onto Simontown Rd. at the sod farm. This road will bend sharply left, then gradually right.
- 10.9 Turn right onto Stockton Bridge Rd. at a stop sign.
- 12.1 Turn right at the T intersection onto Ongs Hat Rd.
- 14.0 Turn left at the T intersection in Buddtown onto Ridge Rd.
- 15.5 Turn right onto Retreat Rd. at a stop sign.
- 17.0 Cross Rte. 206 and continue straight into Vincentown.
- 17.5 In Vincentown turn left at the library onto Race St. to the town's Mill Dam Park for a snack or lunch if you brought one with you, or check out Riviera Pizza to the north. Leave Vincentown by heading north on Main St., passing the defunct Stokes Cannery.
- 18.1 Turn left onto Newbolds Corner Rd.
- 18.9 Turn right onto Smithville Rd. At mile 20.4 use caution in crossing busy Rte. 38.
- 20.8 Turn Left onto W. Railroad Ave. This takes you into the woods again and over to the other side of the aban-

START/FINISH

MOUNT HOLLY

High St.

SMITHVILLE

EWANSVILLE

BIRMINGHAM

38

530

206

Smithville Rd.

Retreat Rd.

Pemberton Rd.

Birmingham-Buddtown Rd.

SCRAPETOWN

N

doned railroad, where the name changes to Shreve St.

- 22.8 Turn right at a T intersection with a stop sign onto Rte. 612 (Pine St.).
- 23.1 Turn left at a traffic light and a T intersection and the WaWa Market onto Rte. 537 (Washington St.). You are now retracing the way you started.
- 23.3 Turn right at a traffic light onto Rte. 691 (High St.).
- 24.1 Turn right into the Fairgrounds Plaza Shopping Center to end the trip.

Heart of the Pines Cruise

Atsion—Chatsworth—Green Bank—Batsto—Atsion

The Pine Barrens in southern New Jersey (Burlington County) is a wilderness area covering nearly a quarter of the state. Federal and state regulations protect most of it from development or abuse, thus making it a popular destination for cyclists. Its virtually flat expanse, the backwoods remoteness, sandy soil, and stark scrubby pines and oaks are reminiscent of swamps in the Deep South.

On this ride through Burlington County (and parts of Atlantic and Camden Counties), you will see areas of specialized agriculture (blueberry fields and cranberry bogs), pass cedar-lined streams, and cross over three major rivers (the Batsto, the Mullica, and the Wading). Canoeing is also very popular in this area, and midway through the route at Mick's, you can take a break and rent all the equipment you'll need for paddling.

You'll also ride through some settlements that feel like ghost towns. When you reach Batsto Village (a former nineteenth-century bog-iron community), owned by the state of New Jersey and the core of the Wharton State Forest, park your bike and take half an hour to walk around the restored gristmill, general store, threshing barn, post office, and the Richards Mansion, once the home of bog-iron baron Jesse Richards. In the summer and fall Batsto sponsors special events. For more information call the ranger's office at (609)

561–0024 or the New Jersey Division of Parks and Forestry at (800) 843–6420.

For information on historic Batsto Village, contact: Wharton State Forest, RD #9, Batsto Historic Site, Hammonton, NJ 08037, (609) 561–0024, or fax (609) 567–8116.

According to Rory O'Rourke, who verified this and several other tours in the book, this tour is thoroughly delightful any time of year. A favorite season is autumn, especially the third week of October when the flaming reds and golds of the leaves usually are at their peak. (Note, however, that the annual Chatsworth Cranberry Festival usually occurs that week, so expect heavy traffic and crowds on that Saturday and Sunday.) If your taste runs more to blooming mountain laurel, an ancient relative of the rose, choose to ride the second week in June. Because the ride has precious little shade, it can be blazing hot at the height of summer; on the other hand, the euphoria of sluicing off the sweat and grime by jumping into the refreshing swimming pool at Atsion Lake Camp may make it worth the hot dusty miles. On Tuesday the pool is open free of charge; all other days there is a fee.

For cyclists wishing to sleep out under the stars, there are two public and two private campgrounds along the route. The Atsion Lake public campground is on Atsion Road (also known as Lake Shore Road) at the start; apply for a permit at the Atsion ranger's office (609–268–0444). Atsion Lake also has cabins for rent. The other public campground is Godfrey Bridge Camp midway through the ride on Route 542 at Jenkins. To stay there you must apply for a permit at the Batsto ranger's office (609–561–0024). The turnoff to the Paradise Lake private campground (609–561–7095) is at mile 48.5, and the campground itself is another 1.5 miles down a dirt road off Route 206. The Bell Haven Lake Campground and Resort (609–965–2827) is at mile 34.8 on Route 542, and also rents boats to use on its lake.

Because there are so few paved roads in this region, automobile traffic can be quite heavy, especially on weekends. Happily, road builders have been busy adding paved shoul-

ders in this area. The only roads without a paved riding area
are Routes 542, 693, 613, and a 1-mile stretch of 206. That
means that 43 of the cruise's 52 miles offer paved shoulders!
One particularly popular road is Route 206, which can take
you all the way from High Point to Hammonton without
going over any major hills, and sections of it are popular with
cyclists all along New Jersey's length.

The Basics

Start: Atsion ranger station near Atsion Lake Camp in Wharton State Forest, on Rte. 206, 10.3 miles south of Rte. 70. Park
in the field immediately north of the ranger's office.
Length: 52 miles.
Terrain: Mostly flat. Traffic can be heavy on Rte. 206 but remains light to moderate elsewhere.
Food: Farm stands, groceries, and occasional small restaurants are at the major settlements; there can be 10 or more
miles between water stops, so take the opportunity to refresh
water bottles or snacks whenever you can.

Miles & Directions

- 0.0 Turn right out of the parking lot at the Atsion ranger
  station to head north on Rte. 206. At mile 3.9 the Sha-
  mong Diner is on your left. Rte. 206 changes from two
  lanes to four lanes for 1 mile. Be careful because the paved
  shoulder narrows to less than 1 foot in this mile. At mile
  7.4 you come to the first traffic light and the sign TO TABER-
  NACLE.
- 7.4 Turn right at the Sovereign Bank onto Rte. 532 (Med-
  ford Lakes Tabernacle Rd.). At mile 7.9 the Four Winds
  open-air farm market on your right offers fresh fruit.
  Nixon's general store and deli at mile 8.7 is excellent and
  usually open. The store in Chatsworth is closed. The next

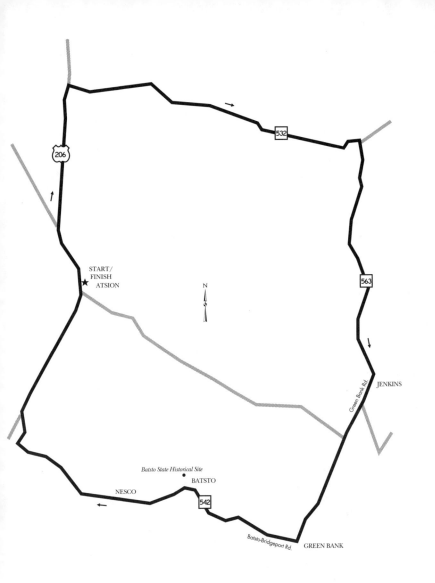

eating spot is the Pine Barrens Deli in Green Bank 25 miles farther on.

- 18.6 Turn right at the firehouse onto Rte. 563. You're now in the heart of Chatsworth. In 0.7 mile, at the cemetery, bear right to stay on Rte. 563. At mile 22.5 you'll cross over the Wading River at Speedwell, the northern terminus of a popular canoeing route. At mile 29.2 expect to cross the Wading River again.
- 27.4 Mick's Canoe Rentals also sells snacks and gas but is not always open. Bear right at the major Y intersection to stay on Rte. 563 (Green Bank Rd.) at mile 28.3.
- 33.8 In the town of Green Bank, turn right (west) at the stop sign onto Rte. 542 (Batsto-Bridgeport Rd.). The Green Bank Inn is a bar that also sells food. However, the Pine Barrens Deli, directly opposite, is a better bet since it is a deli that also sells liquor. Now you're paralleling the Mullica River on your left. At mile 36.4 there is a panoramic view of the water and many blue water (ocean capable) boats.
- 38.1 Turn right into the public parking area of Batsto Historic Village, which has a picnic area, water, refreshment stands open in the summer, and public rest rooms. Ask at the park office about the self-guided and conducted tours; there you can also buy topographic maps of the area. When you leave the park entrance at mile 39.0, turn right to continue west on Rte. 542. At mile 42.4 Farmer John's Food Market in the village of Nesco is excellent. It is a convenience store like WaWa or 7-Eleven.
- 43.6 Turn right onto Rte. 693 (Airport Rd.).
- 46.6 Just after passing the Hammonton Municipal Airport on your right, turn right at the stop sign onto Rte. 613 (Middle Rd.).
- 47.8 Bear right at the end of Rte. 613 (Middle Rd.) onto Rte. 206N. Watch for traffic turning into Rte. 613 and coming at you!
- 52.1 Turn right into the parking lot at the Atsion ranger station.

Pennsylvania

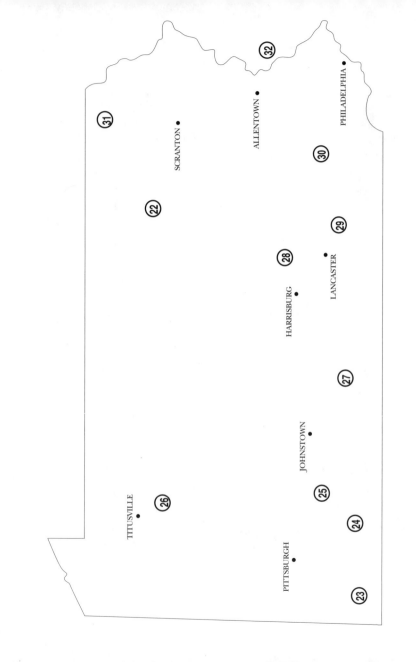

SCRANTON •

ALLENTOWN •

PHILADELPHIA •

㉜

㉛

㉚

㉒

㉙

㉘

LANCASTER •

HARRISBURG •

㉗

JOHNSTOWN •

㉕

TITUSVILLE •

㉖

㉔

PITTSBURGH •

㉓

Pennsylvania

Montour Preserve Challenge

Montour Preserve—White Hall—Muncy—Dewart—
Warrior Run—Turbotville—Montour Preserve

This ride has wildlife, beautiful scenery, exceptionally light traffic, and hills—even a 40-mph downhill. It also has history, as the area is dotted with sites that were used as forts during the Indian wars and the Revolutionary War (Fort Muncy, Fort Brady, Fort Freeland, Fort Boone, and Fort Rice, to name a few), although most of the sites now are nothing more than a marker or a name.

The route, verified by Augie Mueller of Vestal, New York, passes through three counties: Montour, Lycoming, and Northumberland.

It starts at the Montour Preserve, a natural preserve and outdoor recreation area centered on the 165-acre artificial Lake Chillisquaque. The preserve makes it possible to make this a general outing with noncycling family members, who can spend the time you're riding at the preserve digging for fossils in the fossil pit, fishing, boating, bird-watching, hiking, enjoying the exhibits on wildlife, Indian culture, and land management at the visitor center, or just relaxing in the shade with a good book. (The preserve office and visitor center are open all year Monday through Friday, 9:00 A.M. to 4:00 P.M. and on weekends May through September from noon to 4:00 P.M. For more information, call (570) 437–3131 during weekday office hours.)

According to Mueller, this ride is particularly lovely in October, when the leaves are changing color. The first weekend in October, the Heritage Days festival is held at the old Hower-Slote House near the high school in Warrior Run, three-quarters of the way through the ride (mile 29); the farmhouse, as well as the site of nearby Fort Freeland, saw battles during the Indian wars of the eighteenth century. Warrior Run is also worth visiting the second Sunday in June, the usual time for an annual strawberry festival at the Warrior Run Church. And on the second Sunday of each month (except June and July), a few dollars will buy you brunch at the monthly fund-raising breakfast of the fire company of Turbotville, served until 12:30 P.M. in the firehouse building (mile 32).

The Montour Preserve is nestled in the broad Central Susquehanna Valley, surrounded by two, long, rolling ridges: the Montour Ridge to the south and the Muncy Hills to the north. As this ride climbs the steep side of the latter, the terrain is undeniably vertical. The ride's lowest point, near the West Branch of the Susquehanna River, is about 500 feet above sea level, while its highest point on the ridge of the Muncy Hills (at mile 6.3) is 1,226 feet. As a result, despite the modest distance of under 40 miles, it is difficult to categorize this ride as a difficult cruise or an easy challenge. There are so many side roads from this ride that, with a good set of county maps, topographic maps, or a gazetteer, a cyclist can create many variations.

As roads in this part of the world are poorly signed, confusion could easily reign, particularly upon crossing county lines when road names normally change. To forestall such a situation, the map will indicate some of the intersecting roads along the mapped route at lcoations where a rider could become confused.

A note on the terminology: State routes are generally indicated by small (10" x 10" or 18" x 10") white signs along the road; the route number is a four-digit number prefixed by *SR*. Township road signs have many variations. Most are green, but there are a few white ones. Generally, the green signs have a township road number. The white signs are mixed—some have a road number and some do not. The township road number is usually a three-digit number that may or may not be prefixed with *TB, RT,* or *T.* When township road numbers are given, they are shown as the cyclist actually sees them and not as portrayed on the maps. Note that different sections of the same township road may have the same number but different names. Moreover, maps from different sources often disagree about the road numbers. For these reasons, follow the directions and mileages very carefully.

The Basics

Start: The parking lot of the Montour Preserve. From the east on I-80, take exit 32 for Limestoneville and proceed on Rte. 254E for 6 miles to Washingtonville. Continue through the blinking light for 0.5 mile, following the brown signs to the Montour Preserve. Turn left onto SR 1003 and continue 3.7 miles (passing the Montour Steam Electric Station of the Pennsylvania Power & Light Co. on your right). Turn right onto SR 1006 and drive 0.5 mile; turn left into the parking lot of the preserve's office—housed in a restored Victorian farmhouse—and separate visitor center.
Length: 39 miles.
Terrain: Mostly rolling hills, except for a steep climb over the Muncy Hills both to and from Muncy. Some township roads are gravel or oiled-and-chipped (gravel laid on oil and pressed into the road by the weight of passing vehicles). For comfort, a wider-tire cross, hybrid, or mountain bike is recommended, although the ride can also be done on a thin-tire road bike. Traffic is generally light except near the towns.
Food: At exit 33 off I-80 and in Washingtonville before you get to the preserve, and in Muncy on the ride route. Pack plenty of water and snacks for the actual ride, however, as the route does not pass any convenience stores (or public rest rooms); off the route, how-

ever, there is an ice cream parlor in Dewart and a mini-mart in Turbotville.

Miles & Directions

- 0.0 From the parking lot access road of the Montour Preserve's
  office and visitor center, turn left onto unsigned SR 1006.
- 0.4 Bear left onto TR 423 (Sportsman Rd.). At mile 1.1, pass the
  preserve's fossil pit on your right, where collecting is allowed.
- 2.2 Turn left at the T intersection onto PA 44.
- 3.0 Bear right onto T 360 (Shupp Rd.) where PA 44 heads left;
  Shupp Rd. is paved here but soon becomes gravel. By mile 4.2,
  the name will have changed from Shupp Rd. to Walburn Rd. Although the number on the sign indicates that the road is now
  TR 431, on many maps this section of road is still shown as T
  360.
- 4.9 Bear right at the T intersection onto oiled-and-chipped
  Fairview Church Rd., whose road number is back to T 360.
- 6.2 Just past Fairview Church on your left, bear right onto SR
  1003. In 0.1 mile, you'll reach the highest point on the ride. At
  mile 8.6, you'll leave Montour County and enter Lycoming
  County. Note the white road sign on the Lycoming County
  sign—the road changes numbers from SR 1003 to SR 2009.
- 9.5 Just after passing T 608 (Swank Hill Rd.) on your right, bear
  left onto SR 2009 just past two large silos on your left. This is
  also an intersection with T 596 (Kepner Hill Rd.), which comes
  in on your right. This junction is deceptive: As you approach
  the intersection it appears as though your road continues
  straight ahead, up a slight rise; that is really Kepner Hill Rd. It is
  not until you reach or pass the silos that it becomes apparent
  that SR 2009 is going downhill to the left. At mile 11.2, follow
  SR 2009 as it makes a sharp turn to the left, crossing the Glade
  Run creek. In just another 0.1 mile, follow SR 2009 as it makes a
  sharp turn to the right. Soon I–180 will be paralleling your
  course on the left.

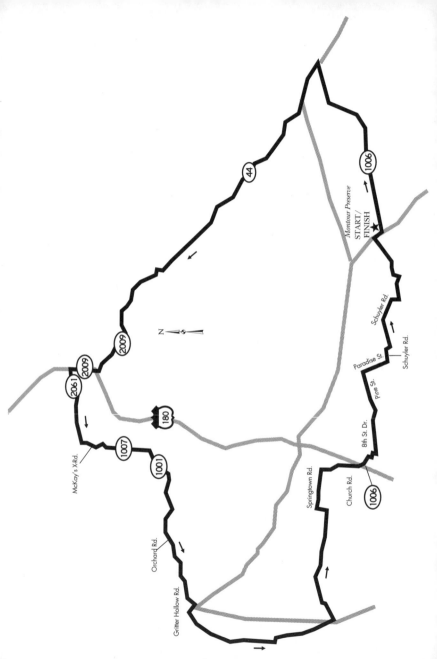

Montour Preserve
START/
FINISH

1006

44

2009

2009

2061

180

1007

1001

McKay's X-Rd.

Orchard Rd.

Gritter Hollow Rd.

Springtown Rd.

Church Rd.

8th. St. Dr.

Pine St.

Paradise St.

Schuyler Rd.

Schuyler Rd.

1006

N

- 12.6 Turn left at the T intersection onto SR 2061 and ride under I–180. At mile 13.0, SR 2061 makes a sharp turn to the right as you enter Muncy. You are now on New St. although it will be several blocks before you see a sign identifying it.

- 13.4 Turn right at the T intersection onto Main St. (SR 2014, also known as Susquehanna Trail), and then make an immediate left onto Pepper St., which you'll follow through and out of Muncy. (*Note:* If you make any detour in Muncy to look at lovely old homes or grab a snack, remember to account for your mileage as you follow the directions). At mile 14.2, follow Pepper St., which will become McKay's X-Rd. (T 432), as it makes a sharp left, a sharp right, and then another sharp left. At this point you are following the West Branch of the Susquehanna River at the lowest elevation of the ride.

- 14.8 Turn right at the T intersection onto SR 2007 (Musser's Ln.). At mile 16.3, as you leave Lycoming County and enter Northumberland County, SR 2007 becomes SR 1001. For the next few miles, as the route dances back and forth across the county line, the township route numbers are confusing. Mueller used the numbers that actually exist on the road signs.

- 16.9 Bear right onto TR 511 (Orchard Rd.), which on different maps is also variously shown as Peach Orchard Rd., T 471, and T 667. At mile 17.1 Bald Eagle Mountain will be clearly visible to your right. In 0.5 mile, stay on Orchard Rd. as it turns downhill to the right; at the crest, the elevation is about 1,000 feet above sea level—the second highest point on the ride. Around mile 19, the pavement ends and you are on a gravel road. *Caution!* Check your brakes! This gravel road is steep in places; at one point you will drop more than 300 feet over a distance of less than a mile.

- 20.0 Turn right at the T intersection onto unsigned PA 54. This end of the road you have just traveled is signed Grittner Hollow Rd. (T 632); it was Orchard Rd. at the other end.

- 20.1 Turn right at the T intersection onto PA 405, and almost immediately turn left onto TR 630 (River Rd.). In 0.1 mile, follow River Rd. as it makes a sharp turn to the left.

- 24.0 Immediately after passing beneath PA 405, bear left to stay on River Rd. where T 628 (Russells Rd.) comes in on the right.

- 24.2 Turn left at the T intersection onto Main St. in Dewart. Continue east on Main St. passing through Dewart; eventually Main St. becomes Springtown Rd. (T 715). Be prepared to follow Springtown Rd. through its various turns.
- 26.7 Turn right to stay on Springtown Rd.
- 27.5 Follow the paved road right to stay on Springtown Rd., where TR 650 (Hickory Grove Rd.) heads left. Follow Springtown Rd. as it makes two sharp left turns, followed by another to the right.
- 28.3 Turn right at the T intersection onto unsigned Church Rd. (T 700); the only sign is one to your left identifying the road you have been on as Springtown Rd. (T 715).
- 29.4 Turn left at the T intersection onto unsigned Eighth St. Dr. (T 705 and SR 1006) and pass under I–180. In 0.1 mile, you'll pass the historic Warrior Run Church.
- 29.6 Turn right at the T intersection onto the unsigned Susquehanna Trail (SR 1007); you crossed this earlier as Main St. in Muncy.
- 29.7 Turn left onto SR 1006 (an extension of Eighth St. Dr.) and immediately cross the railroad tracks. At mile 30.9, follow SR 1006 as it curves left.
- 31.5 Ride straight through the intersection with PA 44 onto Pine St.; you are now in the borough of Turbotville. At the stop sign at mile 31.7, continue straight ahead on Pine St. (A left turn here onto Church St. will take you to a water fountain near the flagpole of the community center. For the firehouse breakfast, head left onto Church St. and 1 block later turn right onto Broadway.)
- 31.9 Turn right at the T intersection onto SR 1015 (Paradise St.). (To get to the mini-mart, turn left instead onto Paradise St., turn right onto Main St., and continue to the end of town.)
- 32.6 Make the first left onto T 617 (Schuyler Rd.). At mile 32.9, follow Schuyler Rd. as it makes a sharp right and then a sharp left, followed by a more gentle right.
- 34.2 Turn right at the T intersection onto SR 4001 (County Line Rd.).

- 34.4 Make the first left onto unsigned T 417; you are now back in Montour County. At mile 34.9, follow T 417 as it curves to the right.
- 35.0 Turn left onto an unsigned gravel road, which is a continuation of T 417 (Gardner Rd.).
- 36.2 Turn right at the T intersection onto unsigned PA 54.
- 36.5 Make the first left back onto SR 1006, at the brown road sign pointing to the Montour Preserve.
- 38.8 Turn left into the Montour Preserve.

Prosperity Covered Bridges Cruise

Prosperity—West Finley—Rogersville—Prosperity

A marvelous old club ride of the 1,000-member Western Pennsylvania Wheelmen bicycle club, this route will take you near no fewer than nine covered bridges. Back in the nineteenth century, of course, bridges were covered in part to prevent the accumulation of snow, which could not be plowed, and to minimize wetting of the main structure, thus prolonging a bridge's life by minimizing rot. Time your visit for mid-September and you may be able to take in the crafts, food, live entertainment, and other activities of the Covered Bridge Festival, held every year since 1971 at many of the bridges. For exact dates, events, and bridge locations, call the Washington-Greene County Tourist Promotion Agency at (800) 531–4114 or (412) 228–5520.

Although the basic ride route does not take you through these bridges, directions are given for a few short side trips to visit them. You may want to do this ride on a cross (hybrid) or mountain bike, as some of the roads on the main route (and on some of the side trips to covered bridges) are dirt—shown on the map as dashed lines. But the payoff is very light traffic and the back-to-nature romance of recalling an earlier age, notes contributor Noel P. Grimm, a board member of the Wheelman. (The ride was verified by Claire

Palmgren of Gibsonic, Pennsylvania.) By the way, these side trips add up: If you visit all nine bridges, you add another 24 miles to the route, turning this 51.4-mile cruise into a 75.4-mile classic.

The ride begins about 1 mile south of Prosperity, Pennsylvania, which, in turn, is about 10 miles south of Washington, Pennsylvania. This tour through Washington and Greene Counties heads north through the tiny town of Prosperity, where a stop at the town grocery provides a glimpse back in history because of its old wood floors, old display cases and shelves, and antique lighting. Then you'll warm up on flat to rolling farmland, paralleling Ten Mile Creek on your left.

About 4 miles into the ride, you'll begin a climb up a 10 percent grade to the top of a ridge—the steepest climb of the entire basic route (although not of the side trips). Once up there you'll pedal along the ridge for the next 12 miles, enjoying expansive views of the farm valleys on your right and left.

After riding through the town of West Finley, you'll coast down into the valley, where there are some good choices for a roadside picnic. The last 20 miles, which parallel railroad tracks, are a slight uphill grade. As this beautiful loop is accessible to most average fit cyclists, it is a favorite club ride and no. 63 in the packet of 150 rides in western Pennsylvania available from the Pittsburgh-based Western Pennsylvania Wheelmen. (It is *very* important not to wander off the road during hunting season in the fall. However, according to Palmgren, hunting is not allowed on Sunday. Still, it's very important to have an awareness of hunting season, and wear blaze orange.)

A few notes about road designations in this part of Pennsylvania: The highways prefixed *PA* have a keystone-shaped (since Pennsylvania is The Keystone State) sign with a one-, two-, or three-digit number. The *PA* highways are also marked with State Route (*SR*) numbers as well as the keystone sign. Four-digit SR roads—which are also county roads—are the less-traveled access roads preferred by cyclists; they can be marked either by black letters on white signs or even by small numbers on reflective tape on a 5-foot-high pole about every 0.5 mile. Roads marked with a *T* followed by three digits are township roads that have little traffic and are usually very narrow; when the roads are marked—and often they are not—the *T* designation appears on a green city street sign with white letters. Having noted all this, "the local people will not know the *T* route numbers, and they usually don't know the *SR* route numbers even though they are signed," says Grimm, so pay close attention to the direction mileages and the map. With the advent of 911 service and its requirement for street names and signs, however, direction-finding is a little easier. Still, one route number may incorporate several names.

The Basics

Start: One mile south of Prosperity, in Washington County, at the intersection of PA 221 and PA 18. To get there take I–79 south from Pittsburgh and then I–70 west. Drive about 6 miles on I–70, passing exits to Washington, Pennsylvania, and take exit 3, marked as Rte. 221/Taylorstown. Turn left at the end of the off-ramp, and make another left onto PA 221S. Then drive about 7 miles to Prosperity, a town with a population of about 200. Here PA 221S and PA 18S share the same road through town. Drive another mile south to the starting point, where the two routes separate. Park on the right (south) side of the road in the gravel parking lot (used for road maintenance).

Length: 51.4 miles (75.4 miles with all the side trips to the covered bridges).

Terrain: Flat to rolling, with a couple of stiff climbs. Traffic is light for most of the ride, although it is moderate on PA 21 and PA 18.

Food: Sparse. Stock up at Jim's Stop & Shop, the only store in Prosperity; other convenience stores are in West Finley (mile 16.4), Graysville (mile 23.3), and Rogersville (off the route at mile 37.5, near the restaurant in Waynesburg). *Note:* On this ride, make sure to drink only *bottled* water; there has been a history of bad water in some of this area.

Miles & Directions

- 0.0 Turn left (north) out of the parking lot onto PA 18/221 (Prosperity Pike) toward Prosperity.
- 1.0 Turn left onto PA 221N (South Bridge Rd.) in Prosperity, leaving PA 18.
- 3.9 Turn left onto SR 3029W (Pleasant Grove Rd.) toward Pleasant Grove. At mile 5.4 don't blink, or you'll miss your passing through Pleasant Grove.
- 8.3 At the stop sign where the road intersects with PA 231, make a quick jog left and then an immediate right to keep going straight ahead on SR 3029 (Burnsville Ridge Rd.).

For a side trip to three covered bridges (11.8-mile round-trip): Turn left instead onto PA 231 (East Finley Rd.). After 2.5 miles turn right onto T 414 (Templeton Run Rd.). After another 0.2 mile follow T 414 as it turns right to Brownlee Bridge (spanning 31 feet over the Templeton fork of Wheeling Creek). From here the rest of this detour to the next two bridges will take you on dirt roads. Ride through the Brownlee Bridge and continue on T 414 for 2.0 miles. Turn left onto T 408 (Hickory Rd.) to Plants Bridge (spanning 24.5 feet over the Templeton fork). Ride through that bridge on T 408 (now called Sky View Rd., and eventually Fairmount Church Rd. Sky View is a very steep climb and descent on gravel and dirt, giving you an idea of the climbs on the other side trips) for 0.9 mile, and turn right onto SR 3035 (Rocky Run Rd.). Palmgren, who took notes and verified this tour from the backseat of a tandem, feels that these dirt roads are too unstable for tandems. After 0.3 mile turn left onto T 450 (Newland School Rd.) to Sprowls Bridge (built in 1875, spanning 27.5 feet over the Rocky Run of Wheeling Creek branch). Return to the main ride by retracing the detour route.

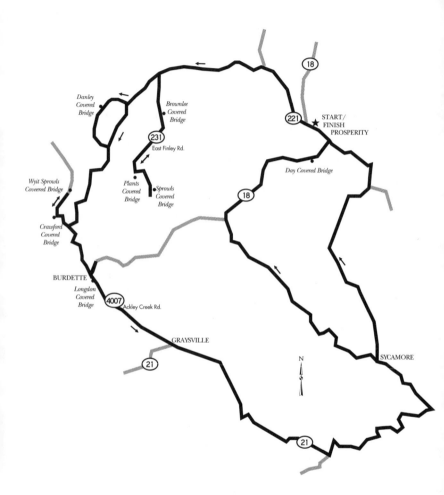

Danley
Covered
Bridge

Brownlee
Covered
Bridge

231
East Finley Rd.

18
221 START/
FINISH
PROSPERITY

Day Covered Bridge

Wyit Sprowls
Covered Bridge

Plants
Covered
Bridge

Sprowls
Covered
Bridge

18

Crawford
Covered
Bridge

BURDETTE

Longdon
Covered
Bridge

4007 Ackley Creek Rd.

GRAYSVILLE

21

N

SYCAMORE

21

- 15.8 Go straight to stay on SR 3029 (Burnsville Ridge Rd.).
- 16.4 Turn left at the T intersection onto SR 3037 (W. Finley Rd.) in West Finley, heading toward Graysville. At this intersection is a pay phone and Scherich's Store.

For a side trip to two covered bridges (4.0-mile round-trip), turn right instead of left at the T intersection onto SR 3037 (W. Finley Rd.). In 0.2 mile turn right to stay on SR 3037. Use caution, as this steep descent has hairpin turns with loose gravel. In 0.7 mile turn left onto T 307 (Crawford Rd.) to Crawford Bridge, spanning 39 feet across the Robinson fork of Wheeling Creek. Return to SR 3037 and continue north. In 0.8 mile turn right onto T 360 (Robinson Run Rd.). Ride 0.3 mile to Wyit Sprowls Bridge, spanning 43 feet across the Robinson fork. Return to the main ride by retracing the detour route.

- 18.7 The road you are on becomes SR 4007 (Ackley Creek Rd.) as you enter Greene County.
- 18.9 Bear right at the base of the downhill to stay on SR 4007 toward Graysville. At this curve the road heading left is SR 4016 (Enon Church Rd.).

For another side trip to a covered bridge (1.8-mile round-trip), turn left onto SR 4016 (Enon Church Rd.). After 0.6 mile, turn left onto T 414 (Miller Crossing), a gravel road. After 0.3 mile you'll see Longdon Bridge spanning a remarkable 67.5 feet across the Templeton fork of Wheeling Creek. Return to the main ride by retracing the detour route.

- Continue straight at the junctions at miles 21.9 and 22.1 to stay on SR 4007 (now called Main St.). At mile 23.4 is Shriller's Country Store, where you can have a sandwich, buy hardware, or rent a movie.
- 23.5 Head straight onto PA 21E (Roy Furman Hwy., also SR 0021), watching carefully for traffic. At mile 27.4, PA 21E will take you through the village of Rutan; at mile 28.5, opposite SR 4017, look right: You'll see Scott Bridge, built in 1885; it spans

41 feet across Ten Mile Creek on T 424. At mile 30, you'll pass Stewart's Groceries.

- 31.4 Bear left at the stop sign where PA 18N joins PA 21E. In 0.5 mile you'll pass through Rogersville, where there are pay phones, the only ATM on the ride, and Rush Grocery and Video. In another 0.3 mile is Center Township Park, a nice spot for a picnic. At mile 35.4 keep heading straight at the junction to stay on PA 21E/18N.

- 37.5 Turn left onto PA 18N (leaving PA 21E), following the PA 18N signs. (If at this intersection you continue straight on PA 21E instead, within 0.5 mile on your left are an ice cream store and Albert's Restaurant, where you can relax with an iced tea and visit the rest rooms. Then resume the main route on PA 18N.) At mile 39.6 continue straight at the junction to stay on PA 18N.

- 40.7 In the village of Sycamore, turn right onto SR 4029 (W. & W. Rail Rd.), heading north. At mile 42.9 you'll pass through the village of Swarts; keep heading straight at the junction, staying on SR 4029 and follow the sign to Prosperity.

- 45.3 Bear right at the Y intersection in the village of Deerlick to stay on SR 4029. At mile 46.7, after passing through the village of West Union, you reenter Washington County, and SR 4029 becomes SR 3039.

- 48.5 Head straight at the junction onto PA 221N (Conger Rd.), leaving SR 3039.

- 49.3 Turn left at the stop sign to stay on PA 221N, heading toward Prosperity.

- 51.4 Bear right where PA 18 joins PA 221; then make a sharp left into the gravel parking lot at the start.

For a last covered bridge side trip (2.2-mile round-trip), turn right out of the gravel parking lot and make an immediate right onto PA 18S. After 1.1 miles turn left onto T 339. There you will encounter the Day Bridge, built in 1875 and spanning 36.5 feet across Short Creek. Return by this route to your starting point in the parking lot.

Youghiogheny River Trail Ramble

Ohiopyle—Confluence—Ohiopyle

The Youghiogheny River Trail is the southern section of a multipurpose trail for cyclists, hikers, and cross-country skiers that, when completed, will be 60 to 70 miles long between Meyersdale and Pittsburgh. Located entirely within Ohiopyle State Park, straddling the border of Fayette and Somerset Counties, this 8- to 12-foot-wide, hard-surfaced path of fine gravel runs through the scenic, forested gorge of the Youghiogheny (pronounced "YAHK-ah-gain-ee" and often called the "Yough") River on the old Western Maryland Railway bed. The nearly level 18-mile out-and-back course from Ohiopyle to Confluence is highlighted by magnificent river views, cascading feeder streams, and maturing forests. The trail was officially dedicated in 1986, after the Western Pennsylvania Conservancy acquired the abandoned railroad right-of-way from the Chessie System and transferred it to the Pennsylvania Department of Environmental Resources.

Although Ohiopyle is nearly due west of Ramcat Hollow, the 900-foot-deep Youghiogheny River gorge carved through Laurel Ridge makes the bike path between the trailheads far from a direct route. Cyclists heading upriver from Ohiopyle, for example, will occasionally find themselves pedaling directly north or south as they make their way steadily eastward. Because it was originally designed as a railroad corridor, the bike trail never exceeds a 3 percent grade. The path appears level on the uphill ride toward Confluence, but the grade becomes apparent after you turn around and gradually descend back to Ohiopyle. The gentle slope and smooth trail surface allow easy access to remote sections of the "Yough Gorge" that were once enjoyed only by whitewater rafters, railroad travelers, and determined hikers, hunters, and anglers.

Although cyclists generally prefer loop trails over out-and-back courses because they do not like recrossing the same territory, the scenery on this trail is so varied and breathtaking that you are certain to notice new features from the different perspective of the return ride. Moreover, take the time to venture off the trail for a short distance to visit the riverbank, tributary valleys, waterfalls, and other hidden wonders just off the beaten track. "The trail becomes almost secondary and a simple highway to the wilder and isolated nooks and crannies of the Yough Gorge," says Paul Wiegman, director of natural science and stewardship of the Western Pennsylvania Conservancy, who contributed this ride

Each season has its own appeal. Riding in April and May reveals migrating warblers, blooming woodland wildflowers, and the river swollen with runoff from winter snows. Summer outings are highlighted by field flowers in the meadows, a river temperature that invites swimming, and the pleasant, pervasive fragrance of hay-scented fern. In the autumn the northern and southern hardwoods on the gorge's high, wooded ridges are ablaze with vibrant reds and golds. For full enjoyment, take a wildlife guide to help you identify flowers, birds, and insects.

Note: As you're heading for the start, on Route 381 just north of Ohiopyle, you may want to stop to see Fallingwater, (412) 329–8501, the famous private house designed by Frank Lloyd Wright. For information on camping at one of the 223 sites at Ohiopyle State Park, call (412) 329–8591; in summer, reservations are highly recommended.

The Basics

Start: Ohiopyle, at the bike trail head parking lot of the single-story frame building that was once Ohiopyle's railroad station. To get to the start, take the Pennsylvania Turnpike (I–76) to exit 9 (Donegal, Ligonier, and Uniontown). Turn left at the T intersection onto Rte. 31E. Drive a bit farther than 2 miles to Rte. 381S, and turn right. (*Note:* This turn comes quickly on a downhill after a blind curve to the left; it is just before Sarnelli's Market.) Stay on Rte. 381 to Ohiopyle. As you enter Ohiopyle, cross the concrete bridge over the Youghiogheny River and make an immediate left just before the gas station, following the signs for BIKE/HIKE TRAIL. Make another left into the bike trail head parking lot immediately off the bridge. If you rent a bicycle in Ohiopyle, you can park at one of the lots in town and pedal back 200 yards to the trail head. A visitor center is one block up the street in an old train station building on the left.

Length: 20 or 22 miles (all the way into Confluence).

Terrain: Flat. No traffic unless you ride into Confluence.

Food: In keeping with the gorge's rugged, natural character, there are no drinking fountains, rest rooms, or eating facilities along the trail. Carry all your own water and snacks. There is a deli in Ohiopyle at the western end and in Confluence at the eastern end (open April 1 to October 10). The Ohiopyle volunteer fire company sells sandwiches, fries, and drinks about 100 yards from the trail head on Saturday from 11:00 A.M. to 6:00 P.M. in the summer. There are clean pit toilets at the Ramcat Hollow parking lot.

Miles & Directions

Note: Throughout the trail's length, mileage posts are on the river side of the path. In both directions, they are numbered one through nine.

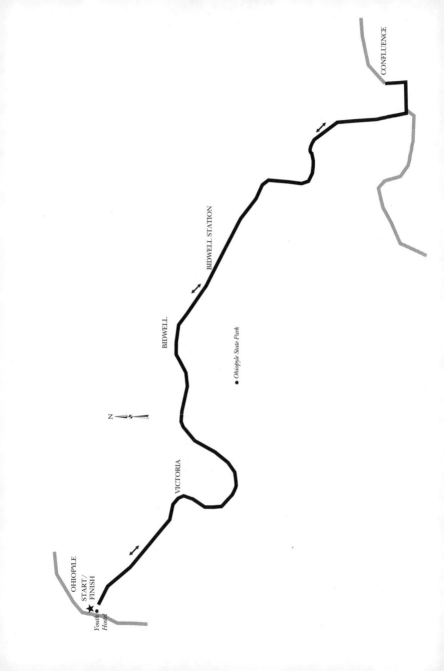

OHIOPLE

START/
FINISH

Youth
Hostel

VICTORIA

N

BIDWELL

Ohiopyle State Park

BIDWELL STATION

CONFLUENCE

- 0.0 From the single-story frame building that was once Ohiopyle's railroad station, take the trail down through a 150-yard tunnel of trees. Soon (mile 0.6) it passes across the top of the wide dirt ramp that serves as a takeout point for canoes descending the river. The path then skirts the edge of a second gravel parking lot (for river takeouts only) and squeezes between four vertical wooden posts designed to keep out motorized vehicles.

  Just after this gate you will get your first unobstructed view of the Youghiogheny River. Trees along the left edge soon obscure the river, and your attention will be directed back to the path as you enter a mile-long straightaway. This wide-open stretch allows time to scan the wooded ridges that tower over the river. All the rugged terrain visible from the trail is part of Laurel Ridge. The section of the Youghiogheny Gorge traversed by the bike path is a water gap carved through the ridge.

- Milepost 9 is at the midpoint of a long straightaway. Between mileposts 9 and 8, you can look into the mature forest for more than 100 yards in several places, even in midsummer. Milepost 8 or shortly thereafter is where the trail emerges back into the sunlight and reveals a panoramic view of a broad river bend interspersed with rapids. Two and a half miles after the start in Ohiopyle, you'll cross a wide bridge at the apex of the bend over Long Run, your first tributary mountain stream.

- Milepost 7, as several other places along this portion of the trail, is marked by vertical cliffs of native stone where the railroad was cut into the hillside. Many have groundwater slowly seeping from the rock, keeping the exposed faces moist throughout the year. In spring these cliff faces are veritable hanging gardens, adorned with wild columbine and earls' saxifrage growing from beds of bright green moss.

- Milepost 6 or just beyond presents a grassy side trail on the left, leading across a field to the river's edge, where a pond-size pool of calm, deep water is framed by rapids and wooded banks. You won't be able to ride a bike past the edge of the field, but the scenery is worth a short hike.

- The area around Milepost 5 includes some sections immediately above the river and some out of the river's sight and sound.
- Milepost 4 is passed on a shaded section of path. About 0.2 mile later you cross an unnamed Youghiogheny tributary. An unmarked trail on the downstream side of the tributary will take you up to a terrace; a side trail from the terrace will lead you to half a dozen apple trees growing wild on the level patch of ground. Milepost 3 is just after some 15- to 20-foot cliffs towering above the path's right side. Wherever patches of soil have accumulated, moss, ferns, and columbine now grow on the damp rock. After passing this vertical wild garden, you'll have views of the Youghiogheny River's rapids and pools of calm water. As you round a bend (after 7.7 miles), the trail passes through a 150-yard-long railroad-carved canyon. The rock walls here rise for 12 feet on your left side and as high as 20 feet on your right. Young tulip trees share this narrows with the bike path, and when in leaf, their overlapping branches create a living tunnel.
- Milepost 2 is in a long straightaway, which is followed by the bike path's most impressive river scenery: a panoramic view of the whitewater-filled bend known as Ramcat Rapids. This rock-and-moving-water obstacle course is a good example of the Class II rapids found on the Youghiogheny between Confluence and Ohiopyle. The steel cables strung across the river directly above these rapids after 8.2 miles are used to suspend gates in the foaming water for competitive slalom paddling. Just before the bend, a wide, grassy area on the path's left edge offers a convenient place to pull off and watch canoeists and kayakers negotiate the tumbling water.
- At mile 8.5 is the Ramcat Hollow Launch Area, the gravel parking lot of the trail's eastern terminus in the Ohiopyle State Park. Cross the first paved road (at 8.6 miles) to continue straight on the trail for another mile. At the sign TRAIL END (at 9.6 miles), turn left onto the narrow paved road, following the sign CONFLUENCE 1 MILE. Turn left at the stop sign—the unmarked position for Milepost 0—to cross the new bridge and immediately turn

left into Confluence, where you will find a couple of nice restaurants. The one I tried was called the Sisters Restaurant. It offers good food at reasonable prices, and the staff was very friendly. To return to Ohiopyle, just retrace your route.

Ligonier Wildlife Challenge

Ligonier—Darlington—Stahlstown—
Jones Mills—Rector—Ligonier

This "Ligonier Wildlife" ride is no. 94 in the package of 150 western Pennsylvania rides available from the Western Pennsylvania Wheelman (WPW), a Pittsburgh-based, 1,000-member bicycle club founded in 1969. The route explores the foothills between the Chestnut and Laurel Ridges in Westmoreland County between Ligonier and Donegal. It also passes near the eighteenth-century Fort Ligonier Route 30 and PA 711.

If you love hills, wildlife, hills, beautiful wooded scenery, and more hills, this ride is for you. On the route you're likely to see deer, mallards, Canada geese, black bears, wild turkeys, pheasants, and other wildlife. Plus there are breathtaking panoramic vistas of the surrounding countryside from the tops of the climbs and colorful wild flowers even into autumn. For those thrilled by rollercoaster rides, on one downhill stretch you can coast at over 40 mph!

Claire Palmgren, who verified this tour from the backseat of a tandem, claimed nothing more than 12 percent. But remember that getting up the hills is only half the problem; getting down safely is the other half. Because of these extremely steep downhill grades, it is absolutely necessary to check your brakes for proper operation before attempting the 49-mile tour. In addition, braking on steep downhill grades requires a certain amount of expertise. So anyone seriously contemplating riding this tour should not only check brakes for proper operation but also practice using them under these extreme conditions.

The 31-mile version of the tour is a cruise for those wanting to enjoy the best of the scenery while cutting off the worst of the climbs.

Many roads are unmarked, and the local people will not know the *T* route numbers and they usually don't know the *SR* route numbers even though they are signed, so pay very close attention to the mileages, even more than to the map, whose scale is too small to show all the intersections that might be helpful landmarks.

The Basics

Start: Ligonier, in front of the National Guard Armory on Walnut St. north of Main St. Directions are from U.S. Rte. 30, heading east or west as appropriate. From the west, drive on Rte. 30 until the first traffic light in Ligonier, passing a Giant Eagle grocery on your left (the north side of Rte. 30); turn left onto Walnut St. From the east, drive on Rte. 30 until the traffic light after the intersection of Rte. 30 with PA 711; turn right onto Walnut St. Follow Walnut St. north to Main St. (1 block from Rte. 30); you have a stop sign. The armory is to the right on the north side of Main St. Cross Main St. and park on Walnut St. alongside the armory. Walk south to the Giant Eagle on Rte. 30, where you can provision up and fill your water bottles in the public rest rooms.

Length: 31 or 49 miles.

Terrain: Moderately hilly on the 31-mile cruise; rolling hills with steep climbs on the 49-mile challenge. Outside of Ligonier itself, Darlington, Stahlstown, and the crossing of Rte. 30, traffic is exceptionally light (maybe two cars in 10 miles).

Food: Several stores and restaurants in Ligonier. Stock up, because this ride is so rural that there are long stretches between convenience stores and public rest rooms.

Miles & Directions

- 0.0 From your parking spot on Walnut St. north of Main St., head one block south to Main St.
- 0.1 Turn right onto Main St., heading west.
- 0.3 Turn right (north) onto SR 1021 just after crossing a small bridge over Mill Creek, which is just after a liquor store and Mobil gas station. At mile 1.9, stay to the left following SR 1021 and head uphill as some unnamed and unnumbered road goes to the right. Watch for deer.
- 2.8 At this T intersection, the ride splits. For the 49-mile challenge turn right onto PA 259N. For the 31-mile cruise turn left onto PA 259S, and ride 2.0 miles; resume following the directions at mile 14.2. On the 49-mile route, after climbing a few hills, you'll reach a high plateau where the Chestnut and Laurel Ridges can be seen.
- 6.3 Turn left onto SR 1008 at the top of the hill. This is a pleasant, narrow, tree-lined backroad dotted with a few houses. Follow SR 1008 as it bends left at mile 6.5. Pass TR 855 (Shirley Rd.) on the right at mile 7.0. At mile 7.4, follow SR 1008 through a 90-degree turn to the left. At that intersection, TR 980 (Fire Tower Rd.) is directly ahead of you and TR 981 (Pluto Rd.) is to the right. Get ready for a screaming downhill. Although the descent is paved, it is not smooth, so remember to check your brakes before starting. (Jim Yannecone, who biked this ride, claimed a speed of 38 mph down this stretch.)
- 8.8 Continue straight onto Austraw Rd. where SR 1008 heads right and Jinks Rd. heads left. According to Palmgren, the sign for Jinks Rd. is fastened to a tree on your left. At mile 11.1, the Latrobe Reservoir comes into view on the right. Depending on the season, you should see mallards or Canada geese on the water.

- 11.8 Turn right at the T intersection onto PA 259S. For the next 0.3 mile you will be backtracking to the intersection of SR 1021 on your left where you rejoin the 31-mile ride. Continue south on 259S.
- 14.2 Turn right at the T intersection onto Rte. 30, riding on the shoulder of this busy divided highway. Fortunately, this fast-moving, heavy-traffic stretch lasts only about 300 feet.
- 14.3 Turn right onto Orme Rd. Now you're riding another loop through a wooded area with summer and year-round homes.
- 15.7 Turn left onto unmarked Clark Hollow Rd. At mile 17.3, cross Rte. 30, *using extreme caution* both here and on the short, steep downhill that follows. Now you are on Darlington Rd.
- 17.6 Shortly after crossing the bridge over Loyalhanna Creek, turn left at the T intersection onto SR 2043 into Darlington. Now you can let 'er rip along a stretch of fast, flat riding. This segment has been recently resurfaced and a small shoulder added. By mile 19.7, you'll begin riding alongside a nice little stream on your right, Four-Mile Run, which will now be your companion for several miles.
- 20.3 Bear right onto SR 2037 to continue the flat run.
- 23.4 Bear right at the Y intersection to stay on SR 2037 as SR 2008 comes in from the left.
- 24.1 Turn left at the T intersection onto SR 2033. At mile 25.8 you will enter the village of Mansville.
- 26.2 Continue straight and slightly downhill onto SR 2031 where SR 2033 heads left and uphill.
- 27.6 Turn right at the stop sign onto PA 711. You are entering Stahlstown. Ride on the shoulder as there is a lot of traffic. In 0.3 mile the 49- and 31-mile rides split again.

For the 31-mile cruise, turn left in 0.3 mile onto unmarked T 421. This corresponds to mile 18.6 of the 31-mile cruise. At mile 21.0 of the 31-mile cruise, turn right at the T intersection onto unmarked T 501. At mile 21.3 turn left onto unmarked T 329. At mile 22.1 turn right at the stop sign onto PA 381. At mile 22.6 turn left onto T 950 at the bottom of the hill. Here is where you rejoin the 49-mile challenge. Resume following the directions below from mile 40.7.

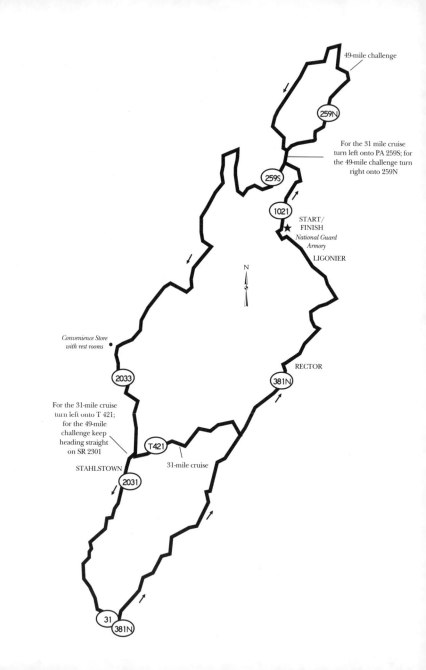

49-mile challenge

259N

For the 31 mile cruise
turn left onto PA 259S; for
the 49-mile challenge turn
right onto 259N

259S

1021

START/
FINISH
★
*National Guard
Armory*

LIGONIER

N

*Convenience Store
with rest rooms*

RECTOR

2033

381N

For the 31-mile cruise
turn left onto T 421;
for the 49-mile
challenge keep
heading straight
on SR 2301

T421

31-mile cruise

STAHLSTOWN

2031

31
381N

For the 49-mile challenge pass the left turn taken by the 31-mile cruise and pedal 0.2 mile farther.

- 28.0 Bear left onto the continuation of SR 2031 (unmarked). Continue straight past the Brass Duck restaurant in Stahlstown at the corner of PA 130 (mile 28.2). At mile 29.7 follow SR 2031 as it makes a sharp turn to the right, going uphill—a climb that is steep but mercifully short. Use caution on this twisting road, which is almost too narrow for two cars to pass each other. At about mile 29.0 is a great view to your left, sweeping down to the Pennsylvania Tpke. (I–76) several hundred feet below and then up again to the mountains in the distance.
- 31.0 Turn left at the T intersection to stay on SR 2031 where Ben Franklin Rd. heads right.
- 31.2 Turn right at the T intersection to stay on SR 2031 (Stahlstown/Jones Mill Rd.), and cross over the Pennsylvania Tpke. (I–76/I–70). Test your brakes, for now you'll drop down some rather breathtakingly fast hills. Remain on SR 2031 (Stahlstown/Jones Mill Rd.) as it jogs right and left.
- 33.2 Turn left at the stop sign and flashing light onto PA 31/PA 381N. Stay single-file on this road because the traffic is fast and heavy. Sarrelli's Market (not your average corner store!) offers food, drink, an ATM machine, and an excuse for a rest.
- 33.7 Follow PA 381N as it turns left, leaving PA 31, and ride through the Mountain Streams Preserve. This road has little traffic and a lot of gravel crossroads, and is a slight uphill all the way to the Pennsylvania Tpke. After crossing over the turnpike again (mile 37.9), you're in for the best downhill plunge of the entire ride—speeds of up to 50 mph are possible. Braking is required on downhills, and always be alert for uneven road surface and gravel. Soon after it flattens out, you'll pass through the Powdermill Nature Preserve; at mile 40.5, on your left there is a visitor center with public rest rooms. You might need it after hitting 40-plus mph on some of these hills!
- 40.9 Continue straight onto Weaver Mill Rd. (T 950 and marked with a wooden sign), leaving PA 381N (which makes a sharp left). Here the 31-mile cruise joins the route of the challenge.

This is another tree-lined, relatively flat road.

- 43.6 Turn right at the T intersection, rejoining PA 381N, and ride into Rector. If you want more snacks and drinks, there is a store on the right at the entrance to Linn Run State Park. Rest rooms are in the small park to the left of the store. Continue past the majestic maples and oaks of the Rolling Rock horse farms.
- 45.0 Turn left at the three-way stop to continue on PA 381N.
- 46.4 Turn left at the T intersection to cross Rte. 30 and make an immediate right onto unmarked Old Rte. 30, just past Marble Ave. Soon you'll reenter Ligonier.
- 48.1 Continue straight at the stop sign onto Main St. Now, you'll half-circle the gazebo in the center of town onto West Main St.
- 48.8 Turn right onto Walnut St. and 0.1 mile later you'll reach the starting point, the National Guard Armory on the right.

Paean to Petroleum Ramble

Oil Creek State Park—Titusville—Oil Creek State Park

Oil Creek State Park commemorates the booming oil industry that once filled the Oil Creek Valley. The Oil Creek Bike Trail, a 9.7-mile paved trail in Venango County that is very popular with families of cyclists of all ages, is built on an abandoned railroad bed with a slight uphill grade going toward Titusville. After beginning at the historic site of Petroleum Center, an oil-boom town of the late nineteenth century, the trail winds its way north through the scenic Oil Creek river valley to the Drake Well Museum at Titusville, the site of the world's first commercial oil well.

With the discovery of rich oil fields in northwestern Pennsylvania in 1863, this area was suddenly transformed into a lively town of 5,000 people. By 1870 there were theaters, hotels, stores, saloons, a whiskey distillery, and an oil refinery. But as the oil boom waned, the town began to die as rapidly as it sprang up, and a fire in 1878 reduced it to ashes.

Today the park's wooded hills look almost as they did before the boom. It is difficult to believe that the valley once supported as many as 20,000 people, that its hillsides were covered with oil derricks as far as the eye could see, and that its air was filled with the raucous noise of pumps and trains and the acrid odors of oil and smoke. The park office has trail maps and other literature, as well as historical displays. There is a parking lot for bike trail users. Opposite the lot is Oil Creek Outfitters, where you can get a cold drink and rent a bicycle from Memorial Day to Labor Day. Call (814) 677–4684 to confirm park office hours or reserve a rental bike.

This ride is one of two (the other ride is 24) originally contributed by Paul Wiegman, director of natural science and stewardship of the Western Pennsylvania Conservancy.

The Basics

Start: Oil Creek State Park office parking lot at Petroleum Center. To get to the start, take I–80 to exit 3; then take Route 8N to Oil City. At Oil City take the Route 8 bypass. After the bypass continue on Route 8N past oil refineries and through Rouseville. Look for an Oil Creek State Park sign (about 3.7 miles from the end of the bypass) and a right turn just beyond. Follow this road about 3 miles to the park office at Petroleum Center.
Length: 19 miles.
Terrain: Flat, no traffic.
Food: Cold drinks may be purchased from Oil Creek Outfitters; rest rooms are at the park office and day-use area at the start; there are services also at the Drake Well Museum and Park, and numerous opportunities in Titusville. There is no water along the trail.

Miles & Directions

- 0.0 The bike trail begins beside the parking lot and is clearly marked. Swing right onto the trail and head into the cool valley. The trail heads upstream on the east side of Oil Creek, and a steep slope laced with hemlocks and tiny waterfalls immediately rises on the right. Watch for a fork in the trail at mile 0.5 where the bike path leaves the road to the left and descends gently to a sharp left. From here the trail descends to the very edge of Oil Creek and turns sharply right under an iron bridge that serves the Oil Creek & Titusville Railroad (OC&T).

■ Milepost 1.0 is followed by a brief rise that will bring you to a bridge over Oil Creek (mile 1.5). Here you have a good vantage point to take in the view of the steep-walled valley, a small upstream island, fish and frogs in the clear waters below, and the active scenic railroad that runs along the east side of the valley. (You can take a 26-mile, two-and-a-half-hour round-trip ride on the OC&T; for information call 570–676–1733.)

As you leave the bridge, you may notice rusting, abandoned oil pipes, nearly obscured by the underbrush—reminders, scattered all along the trail, of the oil industry that once thrived in the valley. A parking lot on the left at mile 1.8 marks Pioneer, the site of another oil-boom town of 2,000. The trail continues to follow Oil Creek upstream, now along its west bank.

■ Milepost 2.0 is passed before you ride under some power lines. At mile 2.8, note the handsome shelter where visitors can rest. Now you are pedaling on a mile-long straightaway past milepost 3.0 through shady hemlock forest. Near milepost 4.0 the trail passes through Shaffer Farm, once a major transportation center in the valley. The floodplain on the west side of the creek broadens once again, and white-barked sycamores stand along the opposite shore. In midsummer this section of the bike trail is lined with blackberries ripe for picking; in the fall, with witch hazel in bloom. In 0.7 mile a clearing on the left offers picnic tables under a large pavilion, and primitive pit toilets. If you're up for a strenuous hike, you can follow the yellow blazes, which start behind the pavilion, and climb to the top of the ridge for a magnificent view of the Oil Creek Valley.

■ Milepost 5.0 is just after the location of historic Miller Farm, the terminus of the first successful oil pipeline, where oil was stored and later transferred to rail cars. Shortly after that is a hiking trail upstream alongside Miller Run that brings you to a lovely waterfall. For the next few miles, Oil Creek snakes through the picturesque valley, cutting alternately into the east and west banks of the creek. The occasional ripplings in the water create a pleasant background sound in the otherwise quiet valley. Groundwater emerges from the steeper slopes, forming small waterfalls along the trail.

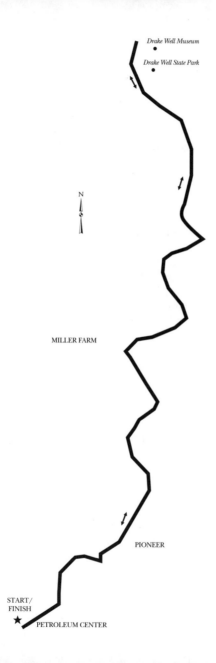

Drake Well Museum

Drake Well State Park

N

MILLER FARM

PIONEER

START/
FINISH

PETROLEUM CENTER

- Between miles 8.0 and 9.0, rusted remnants of the oil boom become more prominent as the trail nears Drake Well Museum and Park. At mile 9.3, the trail starts downhill to the right, with a corner at the bottom. Drake Well Museum and Park marks the site where oil was struck on August 27, 1859, and both the oil industry and the oil boom in Oil Creek Valley were born.

- The trail ends at mile 9.5 as the paved path bears right out of the forest and into sunshine and civilization in a parking lot; the museum is just a short ride across a bridge over the creek. To return, retrace the path back to Petroleum Center. However, I suggest a short excursion into downtown Titusville, barely a mile away along rather sedate back streets. To get there, take the main entrance road to the left for a few hundred feet to the Y intersection. Bear right onto Allen St., which goes under a railroad trestle. Stay on Allen where it turns sharply to the left. At the first stop sign, turn right onto Church Run and cross a new bridge. Take the first left after the bridge onto Water St. and, after a couple of blocks, you will come out on Rte. 8 between a Burger King on your right and a McDonald's down a block on your left. When this tour was being verified in November 1998, there was quite a building boom going on in Titusville, with a shopping center going up immediately adjacent to Water St. It will be on your right as you come into the downtown area from the bridge.

Hanover Horse Farms to Gettysburg Battlefield Century Classic

Hanover—Gettysburg—Rossville—Hanover

Although dubbed a classic, this route through Adams and York Counties is actually a group of three rides that may be enjoyed by cyclists of almost any ability. As the terrain is flat to rolling farmland and the traffic mostly light, the 26-mile ramble is suitable even for novices early in the spring; the 52-mile cruise will delight stronger cyclists midseason; and the century classic will exercise the experts. Since the three rides overlap by a minimum of 20 miles, several cyclists of varying abilities can time their separations and reunions to spend some time riding together.

These three rides, verified by Bill Yoder of Abingdon, Maryland, are based on a route originally used by the Hanover Cyclers club for its annual Labor Day Century. All three routes first take you through the Hanover Shoe Horse Farms, the world's largest breeder of standardbred racehorses, which has produced champion harness-race trotters and pacers since 1926. You'll pedal past a few of the thirty sprawling farms totaling 3,000 acres in Adams and York Counties; the main area of the farm is open for self-guided tours Monday through Saturday from 8:00 A.M. to 3:00 P.M. For information call (717) 637–8931.

The 52- and 101-mile routes then go on to circle Gettysburg, allowing you to visit the national military park and steep yourself in the memorial to one of the most significant battles in American history. If you time your visit for the last weekend in June and the first week in July, you can take in the city's annual commemoration of the battle as well as the annual Civil War Collectors Show and the Civil War Book Fair. Call the Gettysburg Convention and Visitors Bureau at (717) 334–6274 for information, or visit its web site at www.gettysburg.com.

Both Hanover and Gettysburg have many places to stay overnight. Aside from the usual chain hotels and restaurants, the seven-room Beechmont bed-and-breakfast inn (800–553–7009 or 717–632–3013) in Hanover offers afternoon tea and a full gourmet breakfast with—among other luxuries—the option of being served in bed. Right on the Gettysburg battlefield is the Doubleday Inn (717–334–9119), which features a candlelight country breakfast.

Those preferring to camp under the stars also have several choices. Two miles southeast of Hanover on Route 216 is Codorus State Park (717–637–2816), with 3,320 acres of woodland and water offering boating, fishing, hiking, and swimming in one of the nation's largest pools; the campgrounds are open from the second Friday in April to the third Sunday in October. Choices closer to Gettysburg include the Drummer Boy Campground (800–336–3269 or 717–334–3277) at Routes 116 and 15 or Round Top Campground (717–334–9565) at Routes 134 (Taneytown Road) and 15. Yoder wrote that, "The Gettysburg ride is a natural for a camping/self-supported three-day weekend." He suggests staying on day one at the Round Top on Taneytown Rd. and doing a leisurely tour of the battlefield and town. On day two, ride to the Gifford Pinchot State Park near Lewisberry, Pennsylvania, with a stop to check out the Apple Museum in Biglerville (about 47 miles for the day). Day three would involve the return to Gettysburg, with stops at horse farms along the way (about 58 miles).

In this part of Pennsylvania, hardly any roads go straight for more than a few miles; thus, these directions have a fair number of turns. But be patient, for following them will allow you to explore some of Pennsylvania's most beautiful secondary roads. The 26-and 52-mile rides stay within Adams County; the century ride continues into York County.

The Basics

Start: McSherrystown, a suburb of Hanover, at the McSherrystown Borough Community/Senior Center, Recreation Park and Ball Field. To get there from the Hanover Town Square (at the cannon and historical markers), follow Rte. 116 west 2.4 miles to Third St. in McSherrystown. Turn south (left) and go 1.5 blocks. Turn left into the park, where there are public parking and rest rooms (which may be locked).

Length: 26, 52, or 101 miles. The 101-mile extension is long and skinny, with several cutoffs that could shorten it.

Terrain: Flat to rolling farm land. Traffic is generally light to very light, although tourist traffic may be heavy during the peak season.

Food: In McSherrystown there is a Hardee's about 6 blocks from the start at the intersection of Rte. 116 and Main St. There are also many choices in and around Gettysburg. While there are convenience stores in the small towns on the century extension, the territory is generally so rural that carrying snacks and lunch is a prudent idea.

Miles & Directions

Note: Since this is a popular area for organized group rides, there are many painted marks on the roads. Do not depend on them.

- 0.0 Turn left out of the park onto Third St., which becomes Mt. Pleasant Rd. You'll pass the Hanover Airport at 0.4 miles—look out for the skydivers!
- 1.8 Cross Rte. 194 (Hanover Pike) and head straight onto Narrow Dr. (SR 2006).
- 2.4 At the three-way stop, turn right onto Lovers Dr.

- 3.2 Cross Rte. 194 and head straight on Race Horse Rd. (SR 2012). Here the main barns of the Hanover Shoe Horse Farms are on your left; visitors are welcome.
- 5.2 Where Race Horse Rd. jogs right, turn left onto Hostetter Rd. through Allwood Manor, a new subdivision with a stone sign.
- 6.6 Bear left at the Y intersection onto Hoover Rd. to pass Trailway Speedway.
- 7.8 Turn right at the T intersection onto unmarked Sell's Station Rd.
- 7.9 At the stop sign, cross unmarked Littlestown Rd. (SR 2019) and head straight onto Flatbush Rd.
- 8.6 Where Flatbush Rd. turns right, head straight onto Schoolhouse Rd.
- 9.3 Turn left at the T intersection onto Honda Rd.
- 9.4 Turn right at the stop sign onto White Hall Rd., which becomes Maple St. upon entering Bonneauville.
- 11.9 Turn left (stop sign for left-turning vehicles only) onto Two Taverns Rd. where Whitehall Rd./Maple St. heads right.

For the 26-mile ramble follow the curve right onto Maple St. instead. At mile 12.1 turn left onto Rte. 116 (Hanover Rd.). At mile 12.2 turn right onto N. Pine St., which becomes Granite Station Rd. At mile 14.4 turn right onto Low Dutch Rd. At mile 15.2 turn right onto Salem Church Rd. At the T intersection at mile 16.9 turn left onto Kilpatrick Rd. At mile 17.2 turn right onto Centennial Rd. Ride for 0.4 miles, turn left onto Cedar Ridge Rd., and then follow the directions from mile 92.7 to the end.

- 14.8 Turn left at the T intersection onto Rte. 97 (Baltimore Pike).
- 14.9 Turn right onto Barlow–Two Taverns Rd.
- 17.1 Turn right onto White Church Rd.
- 18.9 Turn left onto Goulden Rd., which becomes Sachs Rd.
- 21.0 Turn right at the T intersection onto Rte. 134 (Taneytown Rd.).
- 21.2 Make the first left onto Wheatfield Rd. You have now entered the Gettysburg National Military Park, through which you will be riding for at least the next 2.2 miles. At mile 21.4

100-mile classic

Ridge Rd.

194

Lake Meade Rd.

White Church Rd.

Van Cleve Rd.

For the 100-mile classic turn
left onto Red Bridge Rd. For the
50-mile classic stay straight on
Rte. 394 for half a mile and
then turn right onto Coleman Rd.

Red Bridge Rd.

394

394

50-mile classic

Coleman Rd.
Cedar Ridge Rd.

GETTYSBURG

• Gettysburg National Historical Park
• Gettysburg National Military Park

Maple St.

Bear right here for
the 26-mile Ramble

START/
FINISH
★

Mt. Pleasant Rd.

Taneytown Rd.

2012

MT. PLEASANT

you may turn right and follow Sedgwick and Hancock Aves. approximately 1.6 miles to the park visitor center. Get a free map, watch a movie, visit the museum. You can return directly to the route via Taneytown Road, or follow the auto-tour route (18 miles, you just did 1.6 of it) and return to the route where it leaves the park on Millerstown Rd. For more information visit www.nps.gov/gett/. At mile 24.3 cross Business Rte. 15 (Emmitsburg Rd.) onto Millerstown Road. At mile 22.7 cross W. Confederate Ave. and leave the park. On your left will be the Eisenhower National Historic Site, where former President Dwight D. Eisenhower lived and farmed. For tickets call (717) 338–9114. Admission is only via tour bus from the Gettysburg park visitor center. For more information visit www.nps.gov/eise/.

- 23.3 Turn right onto Black Horse Tavern Rd.
- 25.0 At the T, jog right across Rte. 116 (Fairfield Rd.), immediately bearing left onto Bream Hill Rd.
- 25.3 Turn left onto Herr's Ridge Rd. At mile 27.1 jog right to cross unmarked Rte. 30 (Chambersburg Rd.), staying on Herr's Ridge Rd. At this point, you are about 0.8 mile west of the Eternal Light Peace Memorial.
- 28.1 Turn left at the four-way stop onto unmarked Mummasburg Rd. (SR 3017).
- 29.0 Turn right onto Russell Tavern Rd.
- 31.2 At the stop sign, cross Goldenville Road. At the T at mile 32.4, turn right onto Ziegler Mill Road.
- 33.6 Jog across Biglerville Rd. onto Rake Factory Rd. Biglerville, the "Apple Capital" and site of the Apple Museum, is about 1.3 miles north, and hosts the Apple Harvest Festival during the first two weekends in October.
- 34.9 At the stop sign, turn right on Table Rock Rd. (Rte. 394), which becomes Shrivers Corner Rd. Oakside Community Park (with rest rooms) is just in view to your left.
- 35.8 Turn left to stay on Rte. 394 toward Hunterstown.
- 38.2 Cross Business Rte. 15 at the Distelfink Drive-In Restaurant, which serves great food and real malts but is closed on Monday. Cross over Rte. 15 at mile 38.7.

- 39.9 In Hunterstown, turn left onto Red Bridge Rd.

For the 50-mile cruise do not turn left. Instead, bypass Red Bridge Rd. to keep heading straight on Rte. 394 (now called Hunterstown-Hampton Rd.). At mile 40.5 bear right onto Coleman Rd. The century route will join from Swift Run Rd. at this point. Ride for 1.7 miles and then follow the directions from mile 90.9 to the end.

- 43.9 Turn left onto unmarked Oxford Rd. (SR 1015). At mile 45.3, after crossing Rte. 234 (E. Berlin Rd.), keep heading straight onto White Church Rd.
- 47.1 Turn right at the stop sign onto unmarked Wierman's Mill Rd.
- 47.6 Turn left onto Gun Club Rd. At mile 49.7, after crossing Rte. 94 (Carlisle Pike), keep heading straight onto Quaker Church Rd.
- 51.6 Bear left at the stop sign (Y intersection) onto Latimore Valley Rd.
- 53.9 Make a sharp right onto Braggtown Rd.
- 56.5 At the stop sign (five-road intersection) jog straight across onto unmarked Pondtown Rd. (SR 1006). Soon you will enter York County.
- 57.1 After crossing Rte. 194, keep heading straight on Ridge Rd.
- 64.0 Turn right at the T intersection onto Old York Rd.
- 65.3 At the stoplight in the town of Rossville, turn right onto Rte. 74 (Carlisle Rd.).
- 66.8 At the stop sign in the town of Wellsville, continue straight onto York St., which becomes Wellsville.
- 69.8 Turn right onto Kralltown Rd.
- 70.3 Make a sharp left onto Creek Rd., which eventually bends right.
- 71.7 Turn left at the T intersection onto Rte. 194.
- 73.1 Turn right onto Lake Meade Rd. At mile 79.7, after crossing Rte. 234 (E. Berlin Rd.), keep heading straight on Van Cleve Rd. In 0.6 mile you must turn left, entering the many zigs and zags of the unmarked but appropriately named Tapeworm Road.
- 82.8 Turn right at the T intersection onto unmarked Plum Run

Rd.

- 83.0 Turn left at the T intersection onto Oxford Rd.
- 83.5 At the four-way stop in New Chester, turn right onto Rte. 394 (Hunterstown-Hampton Rd.).
- 83.8 Turn left onto New Chester Rd.
- 85.1 Turn right at the stop sign onto Brickcrafter Rd.
- 85.9 Turn left at the stop sign onto Rte. 394 (Hunterstown-Hampton Rd.).
- 86.6 Turn left onto Sibert Rd. It looks like a driveway, but take heart... it's paved and scenic.
- 87.9 Turn right at the T intersection onto Swift Run Rd.
- 89.2 Turn left onto Coleman Rd. At this point the 50-mile cruise rejoins the century classic.
- 90.9 Turn right onto Rte. 30 (York Rd.) and immediately turn left onto Centennial Rd.
- 92.4 Cross Kilpatrick Rd. At this point the 26-mile route joins from the right.
- 92.7 Turn left onto Cedar Ridge Rd.
- 94.4 Turn right at the T onto Fleshman Mill Rd.
- 95.4 Bear left at the stop sign to stay on Fleshman Mill Rd. At mile 95.6 head straight onto Kohler Mill Rd. At the stop sign at mile 96.6 keep heading straight onto Irishtown Rd. At mile 97.3 keep heading straight onto Black Ln.; do not follow Irishtown Rd. as it turns right.
- 98.1 Bear left onto unmarked Edgegrove Rd. The historic Basilica of the Sacred Heart, built in 1787, is to your right. Visitors are welcome.
- 98.8 Turn right onto Church Rd, which becomes Second St. upon entering McSherrystown.
- 100.0 Cross Rte. 116 (Main St.).
- 100.1 Turn left at South St.
- 100.2 Turn right at Third St.
- 100.3 Turn left into park. Congratulations!

Annville–Mount Gretna Ramble

Annville—Mount Gretna—Cornwall—Annville

The area south of Lebanon around Cornwall and Cornwall Furnace includes some of the most beautiful and historic parts of Pennsylvania Dutch country. On this ride—contributed by the Lebanon Valley Tourist and Visitors Bureau and verified by Bill Yoder of Abingdon, Maryland—you will pass handsome old stone farm buildings still in use and ride along a part of the Furnace Hills Ridge, affording you memorable vistas of rural Lebanon County. Although much of the terrain is gently rolling, the segment through Rexmont to the Lebanon Reservoir on Rexmont Road has a few short grades steeper than 10 percent that may prove too arduous for inexperienced cyclists. Much of the ride is known as the Tour D'Lebanon Valley, a ride sponsored by a local club.

The first part of this ride out of Annville is through level cornfields and dairy farms. Then you'll shift into lower gears as you ascend Mount Pleasant. The climb offers glimpses of the Lebanon Valley below through the cool forests of the low mountain. You'll then pedal through Colebrook and more beautiful forest to Mount Gretna, where you can gaze at the view of Conewago Lake on your left. As a special treat you'll pass the locally renowned Jigger Shop Ice Cream Parlor, which is open in the summer.

The effort at the climb now pays off with an easy descent to historic Cornwall, a restored miners' village reminiscent of southwest England. The village was built around iron mining and manufacturing. The open-pit mine called Cornwall Banks, the greatest iron-ore deposit east of Lake Superior, was once the greatest source of iron in the eastern United States; now it is filled in with blue water that beautifully reflects the golds and reds of fall foliage. The village's heart was the Cornwall Iron Furnace, which fired and bellowed day and night from 1742 to 1883. During peacetime it produced pig iron, household goods, and stoves; during the Revolutionary War it supplied George Washington's army with cannon, shot, and shells.

Today the furnace is the only completely intact nineteenth-century charcoal-iron-making complex in the country. Pay the nominal admission fee to walk in and gaze at the massive stone furnace and its steam-powered air-blast machinery (open Tuesday through Saturday 9:00 A.M. to 5:00 P.M. and Sunday noon to 5:00 P.M.). Slake your thirst at the Miners Village Store while you marvel at the statue of a miner that was sculpted with a chainsaw!

The final stretch of the ride brings you out of the hills and back into Pennsylvania's rich farmland. Return to Annville, where each December the Friends of Old Annville conduct candlelight tours through the historic town.

Note: Traffic can be moderately heavy around the Cornwall Iron Furnace during the summer when it is open to the public. On a Monday when it is closed, however, the tourists seem to desert the spot; you will miss seeing the furnace and exhibits, but as compensation, the roads are delightfully quiet and traffic-free.

The Basics

Start: Annville-Cleona High School on Rte. 934, just south of Annville; park in the visitor spaces. To get to the start, take exit 29 off I–81 and drive 7 miles south on Rte. 934; after passing through the heart of Annville, turn left into the high school lot. Parking is also available at Cornwall Center should you wish to start from there instead.

Length: 28 miles.

Terrain: Gently rolling, with some steep climbs. Traffic is light along most of the route, although there are brief sections of riding along the wide shoulders of busier roads. Be especially cautious about traffic while entering Cornwall Center and the village of Rexmont on summer days when Cornwall Iron Furnace is open.

Food: Widely available in Annville if you ride about 0.75 mile north of the start; available in Cornwall Center and Rexmont and, from April to October, at Mount Gretna.

Miles & Directions

- 0.0 Exit Annville-Cleona High School following the one-way signs, and turn right onto the painted shoulder of Rte. 934N.
- 0.1 Turn left onto Reigerts Ln. You'll pass residences on your right, but the tone of the entire ride is set by the cornfields on your left.
- 0.9 Turn left at the T intersection onto unmarked Mt. Pleasant Rd., a delightful, narrow rural lane that curves past dairy farms.
- 3.8 Turn right at the T intersection onto Rte. 322W. Traffic is moderately heavy, but the shoulder is wide (although the pavement is rough). Watch for traffic for the next 0.4 mile.
- 4.2 Make the first left to continue on Mt. Pleasant Rd. at the big blue sign for Thousand Trails. Soon you'll begin climbing along rough pavement, and then you'll be coasting through forest.
- 6.7 Turn right at the T intersection onto unmarked Rte. 241.
- 7.0 Follow the main road as it bears left and joins Rte. 117S.
- 7.8 Turn left to continue on Rte. 117S (Mt. Gretna Rd.). At mile 10.1 look left for a view of Conewago Lake. At mile 10.4 is the Jigger Shop Ice Cream Parlor on your right; at mile 10.7 you can stop for refreshments at the Mt. Gretna Corner Deli on your left; the Mt. Gretna Inn bed-and-breakfast is on the right. Here

the shoulder is wide but the pavement is rough.

- 13.1 After passing under the overpass for Rte. 322, keep heading straight onto unmarked Ironmaster Rd. (where the sign says END RTE. 117).
- 14.0 Follow the main road as it bends left and becomes Burd Coleman Rd. Now you're riding through a small development of multifamily stone houses.
- 14.4 Just after you pass the Cornwall Garage on your right, turn right onto Rexmont Rd. At mile 15.0 are the red stone buildings of the Cornwall Iron Furnace museum, where you can begin to explore the exhibit.
- 15.1 Past the museum bear right at the yield sign and the stop sign onto unmarked Boyd St. Pass the Cornwall Children's Center on your left. In less than 0.25 mile, gaze to the right at the lake of Cornwall Banks. At mile 15.4 you'll enter the miners' village with its stone buildings. At mile 15.7 at Shirk St. you'll pass the Miners Village Store on the left; look for its chainsaw-carved statue. When you're done exploring, turn around and leave the miners' village the same way you entered.
- 16.3 Turn right at the T intersection and make an immediate right to stay on Rexmont Rd. At mile 16.7 keep heading straight at the yield sign, enjoying the view of the valley to your left.
- 17.5 Turn left at the brick firehouse and white clapboard church onto Store Ln. Now you'll begin a gentle downhill.
- 18.0 At the T intersection turn left onto unmarked Rte. 419. *Caution:* For the next 0.25 mile the traffic is moderate and the shoulder is below road level!
- 18.3 Make the first right onto S. Lincoln Ave.
- 18.7 Bear right at the T intersection to stay on S. Lincoln Ave. Be careful crossing the railroad tracks in 0.5 mile.
- 20.1 Turn left at the stop sign onto moderately busy Evergreen Rd., which immediately becomes Rocherty Rd. The shoulder is wide but gravelly. Keep heading straight through the traffic lights at miles 20.8 and 21.1 to stay on Rocherty Rd. After the second light the traffic becomes lighter and the shoulder narrower but smoother.
- 22.7 Turn right at the T intersection onto Rte. 241 (here called

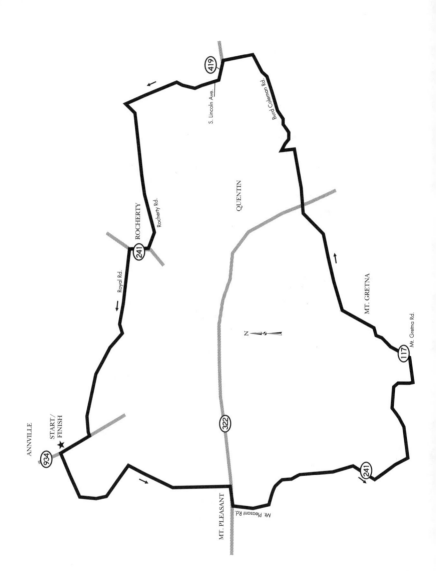

ANNVILLE

START / FINISH ★

934

241

ROCHERTY

Rocherty Rd.

Royal Rd.

419

S. Lincoln Ave.

Burd Coleman Rd.

QUENTIN

N

MT. GRETNA

117

Mt. Gretna Rd.

241

322

MT. PLEASANT

Mt. Pleasant Rd.

Colebrook Rd.), which is moderately busy but has a wide shoulder.

- 23.1 Turn left onto Royal Rd., which has no shoulder.
- 24.6 Turn right at the stop sign onto Oak St., following the sign TO ROYAL RD.
- 25.7 Turn left onto the continuation of Royal Rd. (which actually reads Royal Dr. at this end of the road). Pass the golf course on your right. At mile 26.7 keep heading straight through the stop sign to stay on Royal Rd. (where Spruce Rd. heads right).
- 26.6 Turn right at the T intersection onto Rte. 934N, another road that is fairly busy but has a wide shoulder.
- 27.1 Turn right into the parking lot of Annville-Cleona High School.

Pennsylvania Dutch Sampler Cruise

Paradise—Intercourse—Bird In Hand

On this ride, verified by Mike Vore of Columbia, Maryland, it is likely that you will want to spend as much time off the bike as on, for you will be pedaling through some of the most beautiful Amish farmland in Lancaster County, near or through three of Pennsylvania's several hundred covered bridges, and past plenty of quilts and crafts boutiques.

The terrain varies from gently rolling in the northern half of the ride to longer and steeper hills south of Route 741. Because the farm country is so open and there is little shade, riding could be hot on very warm summer days. Road surfaces are good, but there are occasional ruts left by the wheels of Amish buggies, pock-marks from horses' hooves, and "road apples" deposited by the horses. Although the secondary roads are narrow—usually less than 20 feet wide—the traffic is light.

Film buffs may appreciate the fact that near the beginning of the ride, the route passes the farm where much of the 1985 movie *Witness* (about an Amish family drawn into a murder case) was made; next the route goes through the town of Intercourse, where the fight scene was filmed. But anyone will enjoy the fact that this single bicycle trip will take the rider through most of what is famous about the Pennsylvania Dutch country.

Give yourself plenty of time to stop and explore, for you will have opportunities to take tours of a working Amish farm and house (717–394–6185), wander through the Amish Village (717–687–8511), and watch the animated recreation of a class at the Weavertown one-room schoolhouse (717–768–3976). For more information about what to see in the area, call the Intercourse Tourist Information Center at (717) 768–3882 or the People's Place interpretive center at (717) 768–7171 (both of which you will pass on this route).

You can also eat your way through this tour, tasting the best of Pennsylvania Dutch smoked meats or shoofly pie at the Bird-in-Hand Farmers Market or other restaurants and shops along the way. Should you wish to stay overnight, there are three campgrounds right in the thick of things: Beacon Camping Lodge in Intercourse, (717) 768–8775, directly on the route, Flory's Cottages and Campground in Ronks, (717) 687–6670, and the Mill Bridge Village and Campground in Strasburg, (717) 687–8181. Moreover, there are numerous bed-and-breakfast inns in the area, as well as a few "farm vacation homes"—working farms licensed by the state to host overnight guests, who may help with the farm chores. A word to the wise: Book overnight accommodations six to eight weeks ahead in the summer and fall, which are very busy. Also remember that the Amish strictly observe the Sabbath and do absolutely no business on that day.

The Basics

Start: Lampeter-Strasburg High School in Lampeter. To get to the start, take Rte. 222S from Lancaster, turn left onto Rte. 741 (Village Rd.) into Lampeter; the high school is at Book Rd., 0.5 mile east of the traffic light. Park in the school parking lot on weekends.
Length: 37 miles.
Terrain: Rolling to hilly. Traffic is light except in the village of Intercourse and while crossing Rtes. 30, 340, and 741.
Food: A few farm stands with seasonal vegetables and baked

goods; Amish restaurants in Intercourse and Strasburg. Take water, but save your appetite for the goodies en route.

The Red Caboose restaurant at 14.2 miles into the ride is adjacent to railroad tracks on which the Strasburg Steam Railway runs. Waiting for the steam train, and waving to the kids on board, can be rewarding to the soul as well as a blessing for the feet.

Miles & Directions

- 0.0 Turn right out of the school parking lot onto Book Rd.
- 0.2 Turn right at the T intersection onto Village Rd.
- 0.4 Turn left onto Bridge Rd.
- 1.3 Turn right at the T intersection onto Penn Grant Rd. (Before turning here, look left to see the covered bridge through which you will ride at the end of the route.)
- 1.4 Make the first left onto Pequea Ln.
- 2.6 Turn left at the T intersection onto Lime Valley Rd. (If you turned right instead, in 0.3 mile you would see the second covered bridge near this route.)
- 3.0 Turn right onto Walnut Run Rd.
- 3.8 Make the first left onto unmarked Deiter Rd.
- 5.3 Turn right onto Bunker Hill Rd.
- 6.0 Turn right at the T intersection to stay on Bunker Hill Rd. At mile 6.5 on your right—although not visible from the road—are the farmhouse and barn filmed in the movie *Witness*.
- 6.8 Turn left onto Sandstone Rd.
- 7.6 Turn left at the T intersection onto Old Rd.
- 8.0 Turn left onto Winter Hill Rd.
- 9.1 Turn left at the T intersection onto Stively Rd.
- 9.2 Turn right to continue onto unmarked Winter Hill Rd.
- 9.8 Head straight onto Weaver Rd. (which joins from the left).
- 10.8 Cross unmarked May Post Office Rd. (SR 2015) at the stop sign and continue onto unmarked Lantz Rd.
- 11.1 Turn left at the T intersection onto Strubel Rd.
- 11.3 Bear right onto Girvin Rd.
- 12.3 Turn left at the T intersection onto Summit Hill Rd.

- 12.5 Turn left at the Y intersection onto unmarked Iva Rd.
- 12.9 Turn right at the T intersection onto Paradise Ln.
- 13.2 Jog across unmarked Rte. 896 (Georgetown Rd.) to stay on Paradise Ln. *Caution!* This intersection has poor visibility. (If you turned left at the next intersection, Rte. 741, you could visit the Railroad Museum of Pennsylvania.)
- 14.4 Cross the railroad tracks (and watch for the steam train and wave to the little kids and the engineer). Food is available at the Red Caboose restaurant.
- 15.2 Bear right to stay on Paradise Ln. where Fairview Rd. angles in from the left.
- 15.3 Bear right at the Y intersection to stay on Paradise Ln.
- 16.8 Follow the main road left onto Singer Ave. Cross busy Rte. 30.
- 17.1 Turn left at the T intersection onto Old Leacock Rd.
- 17.5 Cross over railroad bridge.
- 17.7 Turn right onto Vigilant St. at the village firehouse.
- 17.8 Bear left at the five-way intersection onto E. Gordon Rd.
- 18.9 Turn left at the T intersection onto Belmont Rd.
- 19.2 Turn right at the T intersection onto Harvest Dr.
- 19.7 Turn left at the T intersection onto Queen Rd.
- 20.1 Jog left onto Rte. 772 (E. Newport Rd.) and then immediately bear left again onto Rte. 340 (Old Philadelphia Pike). Here you will find the Intercourse Tourist Information Center and the People's Place. If you are hungry now that you are a bit more than halfway through the ride, in 500 feet you can turn right for a stop at the Kitchen Kettle Shops. You may prefer to walk your bike, as the heavy traffic includes tour buses. But forego dessert for a little later in the route. Just a note of warning: While the service station/convenience store is open on Sunday, most other businesses in Intercourse, restaurants included, are closed in observance of the Sabbath.
- 20.4 Turn right onto Rte. 772 (W. Newport Rd.). Soon you will pass the Beacon Camping Lodge on your right.
- 21.0 Bear left at unmarked Centerville Rd. to stay on Rte. 772.
- 21.5 Turn right onto Groffdale Rd.
- 22.1 Turn left onto Scenic Rd.

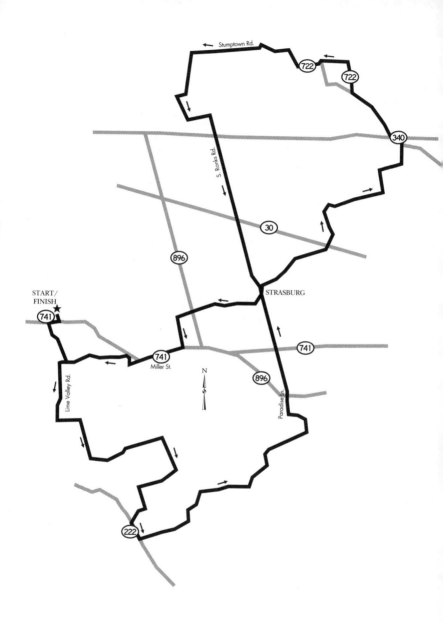

START/
FINISH

741

Stumptown Rd.

722

722

340

S. Ranks Rd.

30

896

STRASBURG

741

741

Miller St.

N

896

Lime Valley Rd.

Paradise Ln.

222

- 22.7 Turn right onto Rte. 772 (W. Newport Rd.).
- 23.1 Turn right at N. Harvest Dr. to stay on Rte. 772 (W. Newport Rd.).
- 23.4 Turn left at Hess Rd. to stay on Rte. 772 (Newport Rd.).
- 24.0 Turn left onto Stumptown Rd. The Mascot Roller Mill at this corner is open from May through October, Monday through Saturday 9:00 A.M. to 4:00 P.M.
- 25.4 Turn left onto Gibbons Rd. At mile 25.8 you can now pick up dessert at the Bird-in-Hand Bake Shop on your right.
- 26.4 Turn left at the T intersection onto Beechdale Rd.
- 26.9 Turn left onto Church Rd.
- 27.3 Turn right onto N. Ronks Rd. Cross Rte. 340 (Old Philadelphia Pike). The Weavertown one-room schoolhouse is to your left but cannot be seen from the road. Cross Rte. 30 onto S. Ronks Rd.
- 30.5 Pass Herr Rd.
- 30.7 At stop sign turn right onto unmarked Fairview Rd.
- 30.8 Bear right to stay on Fairview Rd.
- 31.0 Turn right onto N. Star Rd. (SR 2038).
- 32.6 Turn left onto Jackson Rd.
- 33.2 Turn right onto W. Main St. and immediately bear left at the Y intersection onto Rte. 741 (Miller St.).
- 34.0 Keep heading straight onto Lime Valley Rd. where Rte. 741 heads right.
- 34.2 Turn right at the T intersection onto Hagers Rd.
- 34.5 Continue straight at the cemetery onto Penn Grant Rd.
- 35.6 Pass through the covered bridge over Pequea Creek and turn right onto Bridge Rd.
- 36.5 Right at the T intersection onto unmarked Village Rd.
- 36.7 Left onto Book Rd. and left into the parking lot of Lampeter-Strasburg High School.

Hopewell–Daniel Boone Classic

Kutztown—Oley—Birdsboro—French Creek State Park—Hopewell Furnace National Historic Site—Daniel Boone Homestead—Stowe—Earlville—Kutztown

Berks County, although barely an hour from Philadelphia, is overwhelmingly rural. Undoubtedly, that is due to the influence of the German immigrants who settled the area in the late 1600s and became known as the Pennsylvania Dutch. On many of these country roads, the traffic is light, and it is not uncommon to see Amish residents driving horse-drawn carriages, as they have done for more than a century. In late June and early July, lilies are in bloom, adding a bright splash of orange to the landscape. Several of the roads are positively roller-coaster rides, swooping downhill past farms selling corn or apples and cider (depending on the time of year). You will pedal through rolling farmland dotted with covered bridges and grazing sheep, interspersed with stone barns and houses dating back two centuries. In fact, one of this ride's charms is the way a road may suddenly narrow and then wind and squeeze between the buildings of a farm. The lovely valleys are separated by wooded hills, some of which will challenge the most seasoned cyclist. And throughout the ride keep your ears open for the musical splashing of water in stony creek beds. If you time your visit for Independence Day, near the start you can listen to some of the nation's best folk and country-western singers at the annual Kutztown Folk Festival. And any Saturday in Kutztown, take a moment to stroll through Reninger's Antiques Market to survey the offerings of the area's largest collection of antiques dealers. Take your camera, as this ride features a special treat: It takes you through two 150-year-old covered bridges whose main structures are supported by curved wooden beams—a method known as Burr Arch Construction, named after Theodore Burr, a renowned nineteenth-century designer of covered bridges. The Daniel Boone Homestead, settled in 1730, is the birthplace and boyhood home of one of America's best-known pioneers. For a modest admission fee, you can learn about the saga of the region's settlers; you can also refill your water bottles at the public rest rooms in the visitor center.

The homestead is open Tuesday through Saturday from 9:00 A.M. to 5:00 P.M. and Sunday from noon to 5:00 P.M; it is closed Monday except during summer from Memorial Day to Labor Day. For more information call (610) 582–4900. If you are an American history buff, you should particularly enjoy this ride, for a bit less than halfway through the route, you can stop at Hopewell Furnace National Historic Site (215) 582–8773, an iron-making village that cast cannon and shot for the Revolutionary War and then reached its peak making everything from kettles to machinery during the Industrial Revolution. Stop at the visitor center not only to browse through its excellent selection of books on early iron-making but also, as a bonus in autumn, to get a permit to pick your own apples at orchards near the site.

This ride starts from the campus of Kutztown University (with the u pronounced as in "cook"). It is based on two directions designed and contributed by Mark Scholefield of Birdsboro, Pennsylvania, and verified by Dale Lally.

For those desiring fewer miles in a day, the 95-mile classic can be broken almost in half by camping overnight at one of the 310 sites at French Creek State Park. The route takes you through the campground 42 miles from the start (and 3 miles before Hopewell Furnace). French Creek also offers swimming in its three lakes and 32 miles of hiking trails.

Alternatively, this classic can be shortened to 73 miles by starting south of Kutztown in Oley, a town listed on the National Register of Historic Places for having the largest concentration of stone architecture in the country.

One special note: Directions are given for two alternate routes out of Birdsboro to French Creek State Park. The main route takes you over a hill by Cocalico Road. But Scholefield's original directions included an option along a 2-mile stretch of abandoned road outside Birdsboro that was partly washed out by flooding in the early 1980s and has been blocked off to traffic ever since. According to local residents, the reason the road has not been repaired is primarily that people in the area do not want it to be: They too much enjoy jogging, walking, and cycling along its quiet, forested, pine-scented length. Despite the gates locking out traffic, it is still a public road open to pedestrians and non-motorized vehicles. If you choose to pedal this traffic-free stretch of abandoned road (thus subtracting a mile from the distance of either route), stay close to the center double line since the edges of the road in several sections have fallen into the river below.

The Basics

Start: Kutztown, at Kutztown University. To get to the start from I–78, take exit 12 onto Rte. 737S directly into the heart of Kutztown; from Rte. 222 take the exit for Rte. 737S. Turn right onto Main St. and drive straight to the entrance of the university. Turn right onto College Blvd. and immediately left into the Student Union parking lot. The alternate start is at King's Market at Friedensburg Rd. and Memorial Hwy. (Rte. 73) in Oley. Please park at the far end of the lot, which is covered by gravel. To get here, continue south from Kutztown by following the directions below for the first 14.5 miles, which is the most direct route.

Length: 73 or 95 miles; subtract 1 mile from either if you take the alternate route using the abandoned road outside Birdsboro.

Terrain: Rolling to moderately hilly. Traffic is generally moderately light to very light, but heavier in Kutztown, Oley, and Stowe (a suburb of Pottstown) and at the crossings of major highways.

Food: Plenty of options in Kutztown, Oley, and Stowe; elsewhere convenience stores are about every 10 to 15 miles along the route.

Miles & Directions

The directions below start from the Student Union parking lot at Kutztown University. If you are starting instead from King's Market at Oley for the 73-mile ride, turn right out of the market onto Friedensburg Rd., and you're already on the main route. Continue the directions below at mile 16.6 (the left turn onto Wiest School Rd., 1.7 miles from King's).

- 0.0 Turn right out of the Kutztown Student Union parking lot onto College Blvd.
- 0.1 Head straight through the traffic light onto Normal Ave., passing the university's main entrance. Normal Ave. is a gentle downhill that will take you through four stop signs and past Kutztown Elementary School.
- 1.2 After crossing over the railroad tracks, keep heading straight onto Kohler Rd. Now just follow this road's double yellow line through all its ninety-degree turns to the first stop sign.
- 5.0 Turn right at the stop sign onto Old Bowers Rd.
- 5.3 Turn left at the T intersection onto Bowers Rd. at the Bowers Hotel. At mile 5.4 continue straight at the stop sign to stay on Bowers Rd. and begin climbing.
- 6.7 Turn left at the stop sign at the end onto unmarked Lyons Rd.
- 7.0 Turn right onto Forgedale Rd. At mile 9.1 head straight at the stop sign to stay on Forgedale Rd.; Boyer's Market is a con-

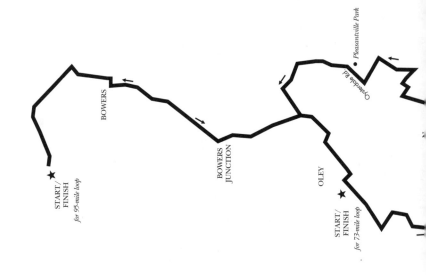

START /
FINISH
for 95-mile loop

BOWERS

BOWERS
JUNCTION

OLEY

START /
FINISH
for 73-mile loop

Pleasantville Park

Oysterdale Rd.

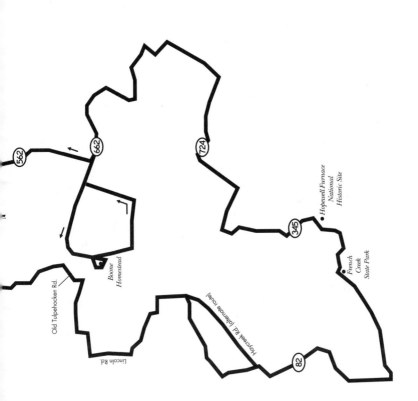

562

662

724

345

Hopewell Furnace
National
Historic Site

French
Creek
State Park

Boone
Homestead

Old Tulpehocken Rd.

Lincoln Rd.

Hopcreek Rd. (alternate route)

82

venience store at this intersection. At mile 11.1 continue straight at the stop sign to stay on Forgedale Rd.

- 11.5 Bear left onto Hoch Rd.
- 12.1 Bear right onto Jefferson St.
- 12.5 Turn right at the T intersection onto Mud Run Rd., and then make an immediate left to continue on Jefferson St. Soon you will enter Oley.
- 14.3 Turn right at the stop sign onto Main St. in Oley.
- 14.7 Turn left at the stop sign onto Friedensburg Rd. At mile 14.9, you will pass King's Market on your right. The 73-mile classic joins the 95-mile classic at this point. In Oley you will find rest rooms, food stores, water, and restaurants; the next opportunity is in 15 miles.
- 16.6 Turn left onto School Rd.
- 17.1 Turn right at the T intersection onto Wiest (*not* West) School Rd. (where Moravian School Rd. heads left).
- 17.6 Follow the main road right (where Quarry Rd. goes straight) onto the continuation of School Rd.
- 18.1 Turn left at the T intersection onto Limekiln Rd.
- 19.2 Turn left at the T intersection onto Oley Turnpike Rd.
- 19.3 Turn right onto the continuation of Limekiln Rd.
- 19.7 Turn right onto Oley Line Rd. In 0.3 mile you will pass a stone marker on your right on the grounds of Hidden Valley Farm noting that it is the original site of the log cabin of George Boone III, Daniel Boone's father.
- 20.6 Turn left at the Y intersection to stay on Oley Line Rd. (where Loder Rd. heads left). In less than 0.4 mile, you will pass Wegman's Deli on your right. Unfortunately Wegman's does not sell sandwiches, only the fixings.
- 21.5 Head straight at the stop sign (crossing Rte. 562) onto Old Tulpehocken Rd.
- 21.7 Turn right onto Friends Rd. Soon you will pass under high-tension power lines.
- 22.4 Turn left at the T intersection onto Daniel Boone Rd.
- 22.5 Turn right onto Pineland Rd.
- 22.8 Turn right onto Troxel Rd.
- 23.4 Turn left at the T intersection onto Schoffers Rd.

- 24.4 Bear left at the Y intersection, following the double yellow line onto Rugby Rd. (where Schoffers Rd. continues straight).
- 24.7 Bear right to stay on Rugby Rd. (where Stonetown Rd. goes straight).
- 25.3 Turn left onto Lincoln Dr. into the modern housing development. Immediately turn left at the T intersection onto Diane Ln. Now you will circle halfway around the development and then out the other side. At the end of Diane Ln., turn right onto Fairway Dr., and then turn left at the continuation of Lincoln Dr.
- 25.8 Head straight through the traffic light (crossing Rte. 422) onto Lincoln Rd. (There are a number of food places at this intersection.) Keep following the double yellow line of Lincoln Rd. through all its ninety-degree turns. Now you're riding through commercial suburbia, with somewhat more traffic.
- 28.8 Turn right at the stop sign onto Rte. 82S, taking the bridge over the railroad tracks. Watch for potholes!
- 29.1 Continue straight through the traffic light to stay on the former Rte. 82, now called Furnace St. Use caution while passing over the railroad tracks at mile 29.4. After passing through downtown Birdsboro, the road becomes Haycreek Rd.
- 29.7 Bear right at the Y intersection onto Cocalico Rd. If instead you want to ride the stretch of abandoned road (the alternative shown as a dashed line on the map), bear left at the T intersection instead to stay on Haycreek Rd. At mile 30.2. you can stop for a snack at the Birdsboro Rustic Picnic Area on your right. Just beyond the picnic area, walk your bike around the gate to continue on the closed road. At mile 31.6 walk your bike around the second gate to resume riding on opened road. At mile 32.6 turn left to stay on Rte. 82 where Rock Hollow Rd. heads right; here you resume riding on the main route. At various turns keep following the signs for Rte. 82. Pick up the directions below at mile 38.7, the left turn onto Elverson Rd.
- 30.0 Bear right at the Y intersection (stop sign) to stay on Cocalico Rd.
- 30.3 Bear left at the Y intersection to stay on Cocalico Rd. Gear down for this steep climb.
- 32.5 Turn left onto Rock Hollow Rd. for a steep, curvy downhill.

- 33.6 Head straight at the stop sign onto Rte. 82S.
- 33.7 Turn right at the T intersection to stay on Rte. 82S.
- 38.7 Turn left at the stop sign onto Elverson Rd. to stay on Rte. 82S. (If you took the abandoned road, resume following the directions at this turn.)
- 39.0 Bear left at the Y intersection onto Hopewell Rd.
- 41.4 Head straight onto Park Rd. (where Pineswamp Rd. heads right). At mile 42.1 you will pass a sign for French Creek State Park. At mile 42.4 keep heading straight past the sign for Hopewell Furnace National Historic Site. At mile 42.6 you will enter French Creek State Park. At the park headquarters on your right, you will find soda machines, drinking water, and rest rooms. When departing, backtrack 0.2 mile to the sign for Hopewell Furnace National Historic Site.
- 42.9 Turn left at the sign for Hopewell Furnace National Historic Site onto unmarked Park Rd.; watch for potholes!
- 44.1 Turn left at the T intersection onto Rte. 345N, leaving French Creek State Park. A tenth of a mile up this road is French Creek General Store, open in the summer. At mile 45.5 is the Hopewell Furnace National Historic Site on your left; the visitor center is about 0.25 mile up the road. When you leave the site by this entrance, turn left to continue the ride on Rte. 345N.
- 46.4 Turn right at the top of the hill onto Shed Rd. Now you will begin a long, gentle descent.
- 48.5 Turn right at the T intersection onto Red Corner Rd. Continue descending.
- 49.8 Turn left to stay on Red Corner Rd. (where Salanek Rd. heads right). In 0.75 mile you will pass the Blackwood Golf Course clubhouse and driving range. At the clubhouse is a restaurant, along with water and rest rooms. Continue the long, gentle downhill.
- 51.3 Turn right at the T intersection onto Rte. 724. Soon you will be paralleling the Schuylkill River.
- 52.0 Turn left onto unmarked River Bridge Rd. following the sign to Douglassville, to cross the Schuylkill River.
- 52.2 Just after the bridge turn right onto unmarked Old Philadelphia Pike.

- 54.1 Turn left onto S. Grosstown Rd., crossing the bridge over the railroad tracks.
- 54.4 Continue straight through the traffic light (across High St.) onto Grosstown Rd.
- 56.2 Turn left at the T intersection onto Manatawny St.
- 56.7 Turn right onto Colebrookdale Rd.
- 57.2 Turn left onto Pine Forge Rd. Use caution on the downhill; there's a stop sign right at the bottom.
- 57.8 Turn left at the T intersection to stay on Pine Forge Rd. (Grist Mill Rd. goes right.) Cross the bridge over beautiful Manatawny Creek.
- 59.0 Turn right at the T intersection onto unmarked Douglass Dr. Now you are riding through open fields and apple orchards.
- 60.2 Turn left onto Fancy Hill Rd.
- 60.6 Turn left onto Levengood Rd., past dairy farms.
- 61.0 Turn left to stay on Levengood Rd. (where Worman Rd. goes straight). Now you will descend steeply into the forest, cross a bridge over Manatawny Creek, and climb back out.
- 62.7 Turn left at the T intersection onto Blacksmith Rd.
- 62.8 Turn right at the T intersection onto Rte. 662 (Old Swede Rd.) and then bear left onto Weavertown Rd., which at mile 65.8 becomes Daniel Boone Rd. Keep heading straight on the main Daniel Boone Rd. where a smaller Daniel Boone Rd. heads right. (Yes, there is indeed a signpost showing the intersection of Daniel Boone Rd. and Daniel Boone Rd.) At mile 67.3 on the right is the entrance to the Daniel Boone Homestead. After your visit turn left out of the homestead to retrace 0.3 mile back along Daniel Boone Rd.
- 67.6 Turn right onto Valley Rd.
- 69.0 Turn left at the T intersection onto Monocacy Hill Rd.
- 69.6 Turn left onto Limekiln Rd. and make an immediate right to continue on Monocacy Hill Rd. At mile 70.0 begin climbing into the forest of Monocacy Hill.
- 70.6 Turn left at the T intersection onto Geiger Rd. Now you're at the crest and will begin descending out of the forest and into rolling farmland. This is a great descent: steep, straight, and—wonder of wonders—*no* stop sign or cross streets at the bottom.

- 72.1 Turn right at the T intersection onto Weavertown Rd.
- 72.7 Turn left onto Old Airport Rd. In 0.1 mile continue straight at the traffic light to stay on Old Airport Rd. At this intersection is a convenience store (not open on Sunday), the first food stop in 20 miles.
- 74.1 Turn left at the T intersection onto Rte. 562W (Boyertown Pike), and then make the first right onto Manatawny Rd.
- 74.8 Bear left at the Y intersection to stay on Manatawny Rd., keeping Manatawny Creek on your left.
- 76.5 Turn left onto Fisher Mill Rd.
- 77.2 Turn right at the T intersection onto Covered Bridge Rd. You will now be rolling through flat farm fields.
- 78.2 Turn right onto Church Rd. This is past the second church on your right.
- 78.5 Turn left at the T intersection onto Spangsville Rd. Get your camera ready for a good picture of the Greisemerville Covered Bridge, a striking red-painted bridge with a double Burr arch and an entrance graced by a large hex sign. Ride through the bridge and up the hill.
- 79.2 Turn left onto Manatawny Rd.
- 80.3 Turn left onto Toll House Rd.
- 81.2 At Covered Bridge Rd. here, the Pleasantville Covered Bridge is immediately to your left. After examining the bridge, turn right along Covered Bridge Road.
- 81.6 Head straight at the traffic light across Rte. 73 onto Oysterdale Rd. A sandwich shop and restaurant is at this intersection.
- 82.4 Bear right at the Y intersection to stay on Oysterdale Rd.
- 82.7 Make the first left onto unmarked Lobachville Rd. at the sign LOBACHVILLE and begin climbing. Follow the main road as it bends left to stay on Lobachville Rd. (where Mill Rd. continues straight). Continue straight through the stop sign at mile 83.3 to stay on Lobachville Rd.
- 84.4 Turn left onto Boyer Rd.
- 85.4 Turn right at the stop sign onto Bortz Rd.
- 85.5 Bear right onto Hoch Rd., which shortly becomes

Forgedale Rd. To end the 73-mile classic, turn left onto Water St. In 2.5 miles, turn left at the T intersection onto Main St. In 0.2 mile, turn right at the stop sign onto Friedensburg Rd. and then turn right into the parking lot of King's Market.

- 90.1 Turn left at the T intersection onto Lyons Rd. for a long downhill into Lyons.
- 91.4 Go straight at the stop sign (following the sign KUTZTOWN 3) onto unmarked S. Kemp St., which becomes N. Kemp St. after you cross the railroad tracks. Follow the road as it bends right and becomes W. Penn St.
- 91.8 Turn left at the stop sign (following the sign KUTZTOWN 3) onto Main St., which becomes Noble St. in less than a mile..
- 94.2 Turn left at the stop sign onto Normal Ave.
- 94.6 Continue straight through the traffic light onto College Blvd., passing the main entrance to Kutztown University.
- 94.8 Turn left into the Student Union parking lot.

Endless Mountains Challenge

Lenox—Susquehanna—Lanesboro—Starrucca—
Thompson—Elkdale—Clifford—Lenox

Green valleys, scenic overviews, excellent food stops, and historical perspectives combine to make this a great 64-mile day for fit riders. Alternatively, given the abundance of bed-and-breakfast inns on the route, it could be a two-day cruise for people who prefer to take more time on the hills. The 64-mile challenge through Wayne and Susquehanna Counties can be shortened to cruises of 39 or 32 miles or even a ramble of 24 miles. Note that two of the rides start in Lenox and the other two start in Susquehanna.

The 64-mile challenge, contributed by Augie Mueller of Vestal, New York, covers an area in transition from industry to tourism. From a history of railways, coal, furniture-making, quarries, logging, and subsistence farming, this ride will take you past a buffalo ranch (buffalo meat is featured in the Lenox Cafe), game lands for hunting, the Elk Mountain Ski Center, upscale shops, ski condos, B&Bs, and fine food. The roads are lightly traveled outside the winter ski season, reasonable in grade, and rich in pastoral scenes and scenic overviews—in short, ideal for cycling.

In Susquehanna, visit the Starrucca House, built in 1865 as a railroad hotel and restaurant and now a banquet hall. If it is open (it has limited hours, as it is often reserved for special functions), you will enjoy the food and atmosphere. Even if it is closed to the public, walk around the building and peer into the large windows for a glimpse of the glorious past. The nearby plaza houses several eateries and a grocery on the site of what was once a huge round-house/repair shop for the Erie (later the Erie-Lackawanna) Railroad.

In Lanesboro, inspect the great Erie-Lackawanna Starrucca Creek Viaduct, built in 1847 to carry railroad tracks over Starrucca Creek. Made of stone quarried in nearby Brandt, the unique bridge has eighteen arches fully 50 feet in diameter and 110 feet high spanning 1,200 feet over the sometimes rushing water of the creek. If you happen to be here in late summer, at a time of limited flow, do not be fooled: Kayakers find this creek a great stream in early spring.

At mile 23.5, you will ride over a bridge just 100 feet upstream from an excellent swimming hole (bring your swimsuit!). At mile 33.0 in Thompson, stop for ice cream before taking a detour to ride along a section of a rail trail more than 32 miles long. With a surface of hard-packed crushed cinder, the trail is most suitable for the wider tires of cross or off-road bicycles. (Actually, you can ride the rail trail about 8 miles from Thompson to Burnwood as an alternative to the paved roads between miles 33.1 and 41.1. If you wish an even longer rail trail ride, access it earlier at Stevens Point at mile 23.8 or Starrucca at mile 29.2.) At mile 42.0, as you start riding the ridge toward Elk Mountain, stop and enjoy the vista of at least 50 miles of hills and valleys.

The Basics

Start: For the 32-mile cruise or the 64-mile challenge: Lenox, Pennsylvania, 35 miles south of Binghamton, New York, or 20 miles north of Scranton, Pennsylvania. Take exit 64 off I–81. After leaving the exit ramp, park in the far back of the Bingham's Restaurant parking lot.

For the 24-mile ramble or the 39-mile cruise, start in Susquehanna, Pennsylvania. From the south on I–81, take exit 64 as if going to Lenox, and then take PA 92 north to Susquehanna. From the north on I–81, take exit 68 (Great Bend/Halstead), and then take PA 171 east to Susquehanna. From the east on New York State Rte. 17 (the Southern Tier Expressway), exit at Windsor and take New York Rte. 79 south, which becomes PA 92 at the border and takes you to Susquehanna. Parking is readily available in the large shopping plaza at PA 171 and PA 92.

Length: 24, 32, 39, or 64 miles.

Terrain: Gently rolling. There is one steep climb on SR 2046 from Gelatt to SR 2077 on the 32-mile cruise; there is also a steep climb on SR 2046 from PA 171 to Burnwood on the 39-mile cruise and the 64-mile challenge.

Food: In Lenox, Bingham's Restaurant has excellent food and extended hours of operation. The owner is also bicycle-friendly, Mueller says. Susquehanna, Thompson, and Clifford also have many food options, and convenience stores are scattered along the route.

Miles & Directions

- 0.0 Turn right out of the Bingham's Restaurant parking lot to head north on PA 92.
- 8.7 At Gelatt, keep heading straight to stay on PA 92. For the 32-mile cruise, do not go straight but turn right instead onto unmarked SR 2046—the first paved road heading right—and ride up the steep hill for about 3 miles. At mile 11.7, turn right again onto SR 2077, another paved road, and pick up the directions below at mile 43.2.
- 18.7 Turn right onto PA 171 (Main St.). You are now in Susquehanna, which is also the start of the 24-mile ramble and the 39-mile cruise.
- 19.8 In Lanesboro, continue straight onto SR 1009 (S. Main St.)

as PA 171 turns right. (This end of PA 171 is near the end of the 24-mile ramble.)

- 20.5 Turn right to stay on SR 1009, following the sign to Starrucca. At this intersection, you will ride under the dramatic Starrucca Creek Viaduct. At mile 22.5, you will be passing through the nearly nonexistent town of Brandt, which was once an important center for logging, rail service, and furniture-making, and the source of the stone for the Starrucca viaduct. At mile 23.5, you will cross a bridge over the meandering Starrucca Creek. (Psst, there is an excellent swimming hole just 100 feet downstream from this bridge.) At about mile 25.0, bear right at the fork to stay on SR 1009 at Stevens Point, which is one access to the rail trail.
- 29.2 In Starrucca (another access to the rail trail), turn right onto SR 4039, following the sign to Thompson. SR 4039 becomes SR 1005 when you leave Susquehanna County and enter Wayne County.
- 33.1 In Thompson, head straight onto PA 171. But if you are in the mood for a fun detour, turn right (north) instead onto PA 171 and ride 100 yards to the Jefferson Inn or Rooney's Ice Cream (in the old railroad depot), and another access to the rail trail. Hobb's Market and Stone's Deli are other possible food stops in Thompson. When ready, retrace your route and take PA 171 south, following the sign to Forest City.

For the 24-mile ramble, do *not retrace your route; instead, continue on PA 171 north all the way back to Lanesboro, a net downhill. At the T intersection, turn left onto SR 4039 and ride another 1.1 miles back to Susquehanna.*

- 40.0 Make a very sharp right onto SR 2046, the first clearly paved route off PA 171. It is about 2 miles after paved SR 370 enters from the left. At mile 41.1 in Burnwood, cross over the rail trail for the last time.
- 43.2 Turn left onto paved SR 2077, the first paved road after you pass Fiddle Lake on your left. (This is where the 32-mile cruise

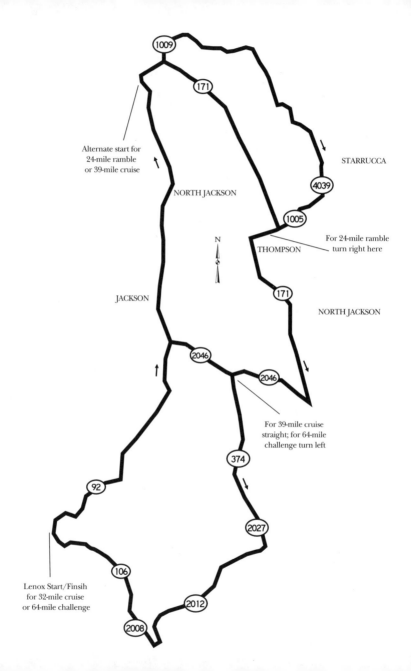

1009

171

STARRUCCA

Alternate start for
24-mile ramble
or 39-mile cruise

NORTH JACKSON

4039

1005

N

For 24-mile ramble
turn right here

THOMPSON

JACKSON

171

NORTH JACKSON

2046

2046

For 39-mile cruise
straight; for 64-mile
challenge turn left

374

92

2027

106

Lenox Start/Finsih
for 32-mile cruise
or 64-mile challenge

2012

2008

joins the 64-mile challenge.) Enjoy the view! You are now running along the top of the ridge.

For the 39-mile cruise, do not turn left onto SR 2077; instead, continue straight ahead on SR 2046 for another 3 miles downhill into Gelatt. At the T intersection, turn right onto PA 92 and follow the directions from mile 8.7.

- 46.0 Continue straight ahead as PA 374 comes in from the left and becomes your route. This intersection is Dimock Corners and marks the end of SR 2077.
- 47.1 Continue straight onto SR 2027 (Lyons St.), where PA 374 heads off to the right. A mile later, you will pass the Stone Bridge Restaurant/Endless Mountain Resort, which has a nice view but few services and limited hours in the non-ski season.
- 53.1 In Elkdale, turn right onto SR 2012, following the sign to Clifford. At mile 54.2, keep heading straight on SR 2012 toward Clifford.
- 56.7 In Clifford, turn right at the stop sign onto SR 2008.
- 56.8 Turn right at the stop sign onto PA 106 (Main St.). The Mountain View Motel and Restaurant (closed Monday) is highly recommended. About mile 60, near West Clifford, just before the junction with PA 374, look for the buffalo herd on the right.
- 64.0 In Lenox, turn right at the bank onto PA 92, and then turn right into the parking lot of Bingham's Restaurant.

Ringing Rocks Ramble

*Kintnersville—Uhlerstown—Ringing Rocks
County Park—Kintnersville*

This ride between Kintnersville and Uhlerstown is among the most spectacular you'll find in Bucks County, with the Delaware River and Canal stretching out along the left side of the road and steep palisades rising above your right shoulder for the first 4 miles of the ride. For the second 4 miles, the canal heads inland and hugs the bluffs, while the road continues along the river. Its beauty and ease make it an ideal early-season ride, as well as a wonderful introduction to the charms of bicycle touring.

The canal, part of a system of state-built public works started in 1827 to connect Philadelphia, Pittsburgh, and Lake Erie, carried barges of freight for more than a century. The Delaware Canal section of the Pennsylvania Canal ran from the Lehigh River in Easton north of Kintnersville to Bristol in the south. Nine years after it was closed in 1931, it was turned into a state park. Now it is open to cyclists, picnickers, and others to enjoy.

At Uhlerstown pause to gaze at the historic collection of houses and canal buildings before passing through the Uhlerstown covered bridge. Built of oak in 1832 and spanning a remarkable 101 feet, this structure is the only covered bridge crossing the Delaware Canal, and it has windows on both sides, affording a view of the canal and locks. Shortly thereafter you'll ascend a steep wooded hill—the only steep climb of the trip, but it is mercifully short. If you must walk your bike, take advantage of the leisurely pace to enjoy the coolness of the forest and the views across the river.

At the top you'll pedal through rolling farmland, cycling past Ringing Rocks County Park. Stop for a few moments to hike out a few hundred feet on one of the trails to this small valley of boulders, deposited there during the Ice Age. The boulders rest on one another in such a way that sound is not dampened, and if struck by a hammer or a thrown fist-size rock, they emit bell-like ringing tones. After leaving Ringing Rocks, you'll coast back down to Kintnersville.

This ride was verified by Bill Yoder of Abingdon, Maryland, a member of the Annapolis Bicycle Club, and should be taken only in the direction described in the route directions; the grades and crossings make it much less safe when taken in the opposite direction. Also, this ride can be taken only in the spring, summer, and fall, as the steep section of Uhlerstown Hill Road is closed from December 1 through April 1.

The segment between Kintnersville and Uhlerstown may be covered either on Route 32 or the Delaware Canal towpath. Route 32 is smooth but without shoulders, and on lovely weekends it has fairly heavy traffic at 35 to 40 mph; the towpath is somewhat bumpy so that speeds above about 6 mph may not be comfortable, but it hugs the water's edge and is free of auto traffic. A cross (hybrid) or a mountain bike might handle best on the towpath's hard-packed dirt, although a thin-tire bike will also do fine. The towpath may be muddy, though, right after a heavy rain. The mileages listed apply to the on-road version of the ride, so they will vary slightly if you use the towpath.

At the start, in Kintnersville, the Great American Grill at Routes 611 and 32 makes huge deli sandwiches of all descriptions, some quite fancy. Take your goodies to go, as the canal towpath is dotted with picnic tables and an occasional pit toilet rest room. There are also pit toilets at Ringing Rocks but no water, so take with you all you will want to drink.

Four miles into the ride, where the road crosses the canal, the Chef Tell Manor House is on your right. The pastry shop in the rear has great gourmet goodies, cold beverages, and outdoor seating with a view of the Delaware River. The owner, Chef Tell Erhardt, is not just bicycle-friendly; he is an accomplished racing cyclist. See if you can get him to tell you how he took third place in a grueling six-day race in Germany in 1959.

If you wish to stay overnight to allow more time for exploring the full length of the towpath, two inns are worth noting. One is the EverMay-on-the-Delaware country inn (610–294–9100), about 1.6 miles south of Uhlerstown at Rte. 32 and Headquarters Road. The other is the Bridgeton House Bed and Breakfast (610–982–5856), just 4.8 miles into the ride. (*Note:* For cyclists who would enjoy making a long-weekend minivacation of riding from one inn to another along the Delaware, the Bridgeton's owner, Beatrice Briggs, can arrange to transport your luggage. Both inns provide support for bicyclists and are within walking distance of good dining alternatives.

The Basics

Start: Kintnersville, at the parking lot of the post office on Rte. 611, just 500 feet off Rte. 32. To get to the start from Easton, take Rte. 611S to Kintnersville.

Length: 17.8 miles.

Terrain: Generally flat to gently rolling, except for one steep climb. Traffic is very light on the second half of the route, although it can be moderately heavy on the first half; to avoid cars for the first 8 miles, Yoder suggests riding on the canal towpath.

Food: Kintnersville and a bit farther down the road; stock up on both snacks and drinks near the beginning.

Miles & Directions

- 0.0 Turn left out of the post office parking lot onto Rte. 611N (Easton Rd.).
- 0.1 Bear right at the Y intersection onto Rte 32S (River Rd). To take the Delaware Canal towpath, use the footbridge 0.4 mile down Rte. 32S to cross the canal, and turn right on the towpath to parallel Rte. 32S. You have several opportunities along the first 8 miles of the course to switch between the road and the towpath. The wide Delaware River will be on your left.
- 3.9 Rte. 32S crosses the canal, which proceeds inland to follow the bluffs to Uhlerstown. The Chef Tell Manor House is next to the bridge.
- 4.4 Pass Bridgeton Hill Rd. The Homestead General Store (0.1 mile to your right at the canal crossing) serves ice cream, home-made soups, deli sandwiches, and home-baked pies and pastries in its rustic dining room or on the patio next to the towpath. At mile 4.6, you'll pass a convenience store that is your last chance for food. On the left at mile 4.8 is the Bridgeton House Bed and Breakfast.
- 6.1 Pass the park headquarters on your right.
- 8.1 Turn right onto Uhlerstown Hill Rd. just after the Uhlerstown-Frenchtown Bridge over the Delaware River. (The Ever-May-on-the-Delaware B&B is 1.6 miles farther south at the corner of Rte. 32 and Headquarters Rd.) At mile 8.4 you'll pass over the canal through a covered bridge that was built in 1832. On the far side of the bridge, turn right and brace yourself for a steep, steep climb of 0.3 mile to the top of the bluffs. The pavement deteriorates a little, but once on top you'll return to gently rolling terrain.
- 9.2 Turn right onto Upper Tinicum Church Rd., the right turn immediately before the T intersection with Perry Auger Rd. At the Bridgeton Township line (mile 10.7, just after crossing Lodi Rd.), Upper Tinicum Church Rd. changes its name to Chestnut Ridge Rd.
- 12.4 Turn left at the T intersection onto Bridgeton Hill Rd.

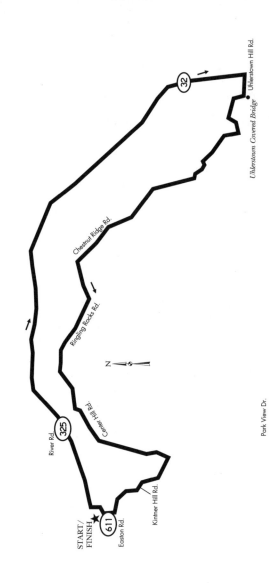

START/
FINISH

611

Easton Rd.

River Rd.

325

Center Hill Rd.

Kintner Hill Rd.

Ringling Rocks Rd.

Chestnut Ridge Rd.

32

Uhlerstown Hill Rd.

Uhlerstown Covered Bridge

N

S

Park View Dr.

- 12.9 Turn right onto Ringing Rocks Rd. At mile 13.2 is the entrance to Ringing Rocks County Park on your right.
- 14.1 Turn left at the T intersection onto Narrows Hill Rd., which climbs gently but steadily; it changes its name to Center Hill Rd. when you cross into Nockamixon Township.
- 16.3 Turn right onto Kintner Hill Rd., which is a winding, steep descent but with fairly good sight lines. Make sure you jog around the building near the bottom at mile 17.3!
- 17.5 Turn right at the T intersection onto unmarked Rte. 611N (Easton Rd.). Watch for traffic as you enter Kintnersville.
- 17.8 Congratulations, you've finished! (Be honest, did you walk up Uhlerstown Hill Road?)

Appendix

Below are some selected references pertinent to bicycle touring in New York, New Jersey, and Pennsylvania. We of course welcome suggestions for new references and notification of address changes. Write to us c/o The Globe Pequot Press or e-mail trudy-bell@ McKinsey.com or velonut@aol.com.

National Cycling Organizations

Adventure Cycling Association
P.O. Box 8308
Missoula, MT 59807
(406) 721–1776
Web site: www.adv-cycling.org

The Adventure Cycling Association is a national, nonprofit organization for recreational cyclists, founded in 1974 as Bikecentennial; since then it has established the 19,000-mile National Bicycle Route Network, for which it publishes maps and marks cross-state and cross-country roads as bicycle routes. It publishes the magazine *BikeReport* nine times a year for members, including the annual reference *Cyclists' Yellow Pages;* sells panniers, tents, guidebooks, and other touring merchandise; and conducts guided bicycle tours, including ones up to three months long across the country.

League of American Bicyclists
1612 K St., NW, Suite 401
Washington, DC 20006
(202) 822–1333, fax (202) 822–1334
E-mail: Bikeleague@aol.com; Web site: www.bikeleague.org

The League (a century-old organization until 1994 called the League of American Wheelmen) is a national, nonprofit bicycle-advocacy organization, serving the interests of touring, utilitarian, and club cyclists. It has a full-time government relations advocate, who represents the League's concerns with legislation and other activities to gain for cyclists greater legal rights and safer access to roads. It publishes the magazine *Bicycle USA* eight times a year for members, including the annual *TourFinder* and *Almanac* reference issues.

State Cycling Organizations

Some telephone numbers are not included, following club policy.

New York
www.bikeleague.org/
mbrship2/clubs/ny.htm

Big Wheels Bicycle Club
4456 Beachridge Rd.
Lockport, NY 14094
(716) 625–8308

Canton Bicycle Club Inc.
P.O. Box 364
Canton, NY 13617
bikectn@northnet.org
www.northnet.org/bikenny

Cruise Brothers Bike Club, Inc.
P.O. Box 456
Copiague, NY 11726–0456
(516) 541–1707

Fast & Fabulous Cyclists
P.O. Box 87, Ansonia Station
New York, NY 10023

Five Borough Bicycle Club
891 Amsterdam Avenue
New York, NY 10025–4403
(212) 932–2300 ext. 115

Contact person: Steve Jackel, president
www.5bbc.org/index.html
Fivebbc@Panix.com

Finger Lakes Cycling Club
1431 Mecklenburg Rd.
Ithaca, NY 14850–9301

Long Island Bicycle Club
c/o Bill Selsky, president
100 South Ocean Ave., Apt. 3K
Freeport, NY 11520
(516) 379–4484
bselsky@cmp.com
www.bicyclelongisland.org/libc/

Massapequa Park Bicycle Club
P.O. Box 231
Massapequa, NY 11758
Contact: Jeanne Anne Braddick
(516) 942–3727
msmingel@li.net
www.li.net/~msmingel/
' mpbc.html

Mid–Hudson Bicycle Club
P.O. Box 1727

Poughkeepsie, NY 12538–1727
Contact: Tracey Donaldson

Mid–Hudson Bike Club
Membership
194 Birch Drive
Pleasant Valley, NY 12569
mhbc@mhv.net
www.mhv.net/~mhbc.htm

Mohawk–Hudson Cycling Club
P.O. Box 12575
Albany, NY 12212–2575
(518) 437–9579
www.albany.net/~kormisto/
index.htm

New York Bicycling Coalition
43 Fuller Rd.
Albany, NY 12205
www.serotta.com/nybc

Niagara Frontier Bicycle Club,
Inc.
P.O. Box 211
Buffalo, NY 14226–0211
Contact: Patrick O'Keefe
(716) 741–4144
chas@net.bluemoon.net

Onondaga Cycling Club
P.O. Box 6307
Syracuse, NY 13217–6307
www.cny.com/OCC/

Orange County Bicycle Club
c/o Deborah White
68 South St.
Warwick, NY 10990–1621
(914) 986–2659

Rochester Bicycling Club
P.O. Box 10100
Rochester, NY 14610
Contact: Todd Calvin
(716) 723–2953
info@rbcbbs.win.net
www.win.net/~rbcbbs

Southern Tier Bicycle Club, Inc.
(Broome and Tioga Counties)
P.O. Box 0601
Binghamton, NY 13902–0601
Contact: Craig Martindale,
president
(607) 773–1512
cmartindale@worldnet.att.net
www.pages.prodigy.net/ira/
stbc.htm
Staten Island Bicycling Club
P.O. Box 141016
Staten Island, NY 10314–1016

Suffolk Bicycle Riders
Association
P.O. Box 404
St. James, NY 11780–0404
(516) 842–4699
www.bicyclelongisland.org/
sbra/

New Jersey
www.bikeleague.org/
mbrship2/clubs/nj.htm

Bicycle Touring Club of North
Jersey
P.O. Box 839
Mahwah, NJ 07430–0839
(973) 284–0404
www.home.att.net/~btcnj/
about.htm

Bicycle Touring Club of North
Jersey
446 Ellis Pl.
Wyckoff, NJ 07481–1836
home.att.net/~btcnj

Central Jersey Bicycle Club, Inc.
P.O. Box 2202
Edison, NJ 08818–2202
(732) 225–HUBS

The Chain Gang
P.O. Box 5118
Phillipsburg, NJ 08865
(610) 837–4884
chaingng@fast.net

East Coast Bicycle Club of
Ocean County
P.O. Box 260
Bayville, NJ 08721
Contact: Rich Baumann
(732) 269–9702
rich@baumann.org
www.baumann.org/ecbc

Jersey Shore Touring Society
P.O. Box 8581
Red Bank, NJ 07701
(732) 747–8206
jsts@erols.com
www.erols.com/jsts/facts.html

Morris Area Freewheelers
Bicycle Club
39 Hampshire Drive
Mendham, New Jersey 07945
George Connolly, president,
(201) 543–4581
Jack Kelly, membership coordi-
nator, (201) 691–9275
www.users.aol.com/atbbiker/
fwnews/maf.html

New Jersey Tandem Club
c/o Team Rutch
231 Brookside Ave.
Laurence Harbor, NJ 08879
(732) 566–9536

Princeton Freewheelers, Inc.
P.O. Box 1204
Princeton, NJ 08542–1204
(609) 921–6685

Shore Cycle Club
P.O. Box 492
Northfield, NJ 08225–0492
(609) 652–0880
www.pages.prodigy.com/
kchf06a/scc.htm

South Jersey Wheelmen
c/o Arthur Schalick
P.O. Box 2705
S. Vineland, NJ 08360–1076
(609) 848–6123
jeffrides@aol.com

The Wayfarers
P.O. Box 211
Fair Lawn, NJ 07410
(201) 796–9344

Western Jersey Wheelmen
41 Philhower Rd.
Lebanon, NJ 08833–4515
(908) 832–7161
www.bike.princeton.edu/wjw

Pennsylvania
(www.bikeleague.org/
mbrship2/clubs/pa.htm)

The Anthracite Bicycling Club
87 School Lane
Conyngham, PA 18219
Contact: Jim Kuzmak
(570) 788–2965
wheelright@aol.com

Berks County Bicycle Club
c/o Rick & Wendy Davis
3727 Patton St.
Reading, PA 19606
(215) 370–5092

Bicycle Club of Philadelphia
P.O. Box 30235
Philadelphia, PA 19103–8235
(570) 735–2453
bikeclub@libertynet.org
www.libertynet.org/~bikeclub
Brandywine Bicycle Club
P.O. Box 3162
West Chester, PA 19381–3162

Central Bucks Bicycling Club
P.O. Box 295
Buckingham, PA 18912–0295
(570) 346–8483
cbbc.cycle.org/default.lasso

Hanover Cycles
129 Baltimore St.
Hanover, PA 17331
President: Jeff Caples
105 Main St.
McSherrystown, PA 17344
(717) 633–7273
Contact: Robert Nordvall
bnordval@gettysburg.edu
www.bucycleclubs.com/
hanovercyclers

Harrisburg Bicycle Club
1011 Bridge St.
New Cumberland, PA
17070–1631
(717) 975–9879
Contact: BillWierman
members.aol.com/mfm2783/
hbc2.html

Lackawanna Bicycle Club
P.O. Box 149
Dunmore, PA 18512–0149
(570) 347–7620

Lancaster Bicycle Club
P.O. Box 535
Lancaster, PA 17608–0535
(717) 396–9299
www.concentric.net/
~Outspokn/lbcmain.html

Lehigh Wheelmen Association
P.O. Box 356
(570) 967–2653
lehighwheelmen@enter.net
www.enter.net/
~lehighwheelmen

Suburban Cyclists Unlimited
P.O. Box 401
Horsham, PA 19044–0401
(570) 628–8636

Tandems of York Society
P.O. Box 92
Dallastown, PA 17313
Deb & Gary Franke
franke@netrax.net or
Joe & Carolyn Stafford
ToysofYork@aol.com
www.members.aol.com/
ToysofYork/home.htm

Two-Tired Bicycle Club
3447 Wilmington Rd., Ste. C
New Castle, PA 16105

Valley Forge Bicycle Club
2003 Bridle Ln.
Oreland, PA 19075
(215) 233–4183

The Wayfarers
P.O. Box 142
Danville, PA 17821–0142
(570) 275–1707

Wyoming Valley Bicycle Club
P.O. Box 253
Dallas, PA 18612
Contact: Mark Hozempa
(570) 675–4866
mehozi@aol.com

Western Pennsylvania
Wheelmen
P.O. Box 6952
Pittsburgh, PA 15212–0952
(412) 782–1341
President: Kathy Smith
wpw96@nb.net
wpwbike@juno.com
www.trfn.clpgh.org/wpw/_

State Bicycling Maps and Guides

The DeLorme Mapping Company has published an *Atlas & Gazetteer* for Delaware and Maryland, New York and Pennsylvania. The large-format book of topographic maps also shows dirt and paved roads and suggested bicycle routes, and it lists wildlife areas and other local attractions. These maps are accurate and are superb in rural areas; their scale is too small, however, to be helpful in towns and cities. For a list and prices, contact DeLorme Mapping Co., P.O. Box 298, Freeport, ME 04032; (800) 227–1656; Web site: www.delorme.com.

New York
Maps of New York counties near New York City can be obtained at many local stationery stores and newsstands; the major local publishers are Geographia, Hagstrom, and Patton.

New York State and County Road Maps
Map Information Unit
New York State Department of Transportation
State Campus, Building 4, Room 105
Albany, NY 12232
(518) 457–3555
Send SASE for complete list and prices.

New Jersey
New Jersey county maps can be obtained at many local stationery stores and newsstands; the major local publishers are Geographia, Hagstrom, and Patton.

New Jersey Bicycling Information Packet
Pedestrian/Bicycle Advocate
New Jersey Department of Transportation
1035 Parkway Ave., CN600
Trenton, NJ 08625
(609) 530–8051, 530–4578

Free packet, including a detailed information booklet listing clubs, tour organizations, map sources, Hudson River crossing information, touring and commuting tips, state cycling laws, etc.

Bicycling Suitability Map of Western Jersey
Dan Rappaport
Holly House, #5M
Princeton, NJ 08540
$7.50.

Pennsylvania
Pennsylvania State and County Road Maps
Pennsylvania Department of Transportation (PennDOT) Sales Store
P.O. Box 2028
Harrisburg, PA 17105–2028
(717) 787–6746
County maps, $2.50 each folded, $133.00 per set, one map per county.

Pennsylvania County Maps
County Maps
821 Puetz Place
Lyndon Station, WI 53844
(608) 666–3331
$11.90 postpaid. Book of county maps with information on history and natural and recreational areas.

Bicycling Directory of Pennsylvania
Pennsylvania Department of Transportation (PennDOT) Sales Store
Distribution Services Unit
Room G-123
Transportation and Safety Building
Harrisburg, PA 17120
PennDOT Publication 316, is a twenty-eight page booklet on bike clubs, annual rides, bike shops, campsites, rail trails, transit company bike policies, and more. Free.

Bicycle Touring Companies

This is only a partial list of locally based commercial touring companies that concentrate their efforts in the areas covered in this book. Many reputable touring companies headquartered outside the area also offer lovely regional tours. For more information consult the Adventure Cycling Association's *The Cyclists' Yellow Pages* or the League of American Bicyclists' *Bicycle USA TourFinder*.

In addition, charities such as the American Cancer Society, the American Diabetes Association, the American Lung Association, the March of Dimes, the National Multiple Sclerosis Society, and the United Way sponsor one-day and weekend fund-raising tours, whereby participants take pledges per mile traveled. Contact your local office of the charity for information about fund-raising rides in your area.

Hostelling International/American Youth Hostels
P.O. Box 37613
Washington, DC 20013–7613
(202) 783–6161
Web site: www.hiayh.org

Brooks Country Cycling and Hiking Tours
140 W. 83rd St.
New York, NY 10024
(212) 874–5151 or (800) 284–8954 (outside New York, New Jersey, and Connecticut)
Web site: www.brookscountrycycling.com

True Wheel Tours
P.O. Box 366
Long Lake, NY 12847–0366
(518) 624–2056
Web site: www.gorp.com/truewheel/tw3.htm
Specializes in the Adirondacks, Finger Lakes, and Catskills regions in New York.

Additional Cycling Links on the Web

On the Web, www.cycling.org has links to many other sites. Also www.bikescape.com is very extensive. Using these sites and the homepage of the League of American Bicyclists (www.bikeleague. org), you should be able to get anything cycling related from bike clubs to bicycle touring companies.

Acknowledgments

I certainly wish to thank everyone who helped me in this, my first commercial cycling book. I still find it hard to believe that I got paid to do something that I really do love to do—ride my bike, develop new bicycle tours, and write about it!

First and foremost I wish to thank Trudy Bell for entrusting me with her work. It was truly gratifying to enjoy her confidence in my writing. Then there were a number of dedicated cyclists who verified many of the routes. This includes Bill Yoder of Abingdon, Maryland, and Mike Vore of Columbia, Maryland; Angie Mueller of Vestal, New York, Clair Palmgren, of the Carnegie Mellon Cycling Club, Mike Rosanio from Manlius, New York; and Gil Gilmore of Norwalk, Connecticut, Jay Carney from Connecticut, and a great big thank you to Rory O'Rourk of Matawan, New Jersey, who not only verified every New Jersey tour in the book, but also supplied new routes.

I also wish to publicly acknowledge the expertise and support from the riders of the Canton (NY) Bicycle Club, who, in addition to putting up with my constant chatter about this book both on and off the bike, provided a lot of useful information about the tours in northern New York. This includes Jim Barrick, our newsletter editor, and our club secretary, Anne Launt, who faithfully read and corrected the manuscript. In addition, Chris Battera (St. Lawrence University Class of '99), who worked for me in the Carnegie Language Center, did a lot of work collecting and correcting the information in the Appendix.

Last but not least I wish to acknowledge the fine folks at Globe Pequot, particularly Liz Taylor, who made it all possible.

—Dale Lally

About the Authors

Trudy E. Bell is an avid touring cyclist and a certified bicycle mechanic (East Coast Bicycle Academy, Harrisonburg, Virginia, 1989). She has taught an introductory course in bicycle touring at the South Orange–Maplewood Adult School in New Jersey and at the Learning Annex in New York City.

Either with groups or solo, she and her 1984 Univega SportTour have cycled all over the Mid-Atlantic states and in Colorado, Utah, and California, including down the length of Baja California. In addition, she commuted by bicycle on the streets of New York City for five years (worth about 6,000 miles).

A former editor of *Scientific American, Omni,* and *IEEE Spectrum* magazines in New York City, she is now a communications specialist for McKinsey & Co., Inc. in Cleveland, Ohio. She has a master's degree in the history of science (American astronomy) from New York University. Her articles on bicycling have been published in *Adventure Cyclist, Collier's Encyclopedia, The Encyclopedia of New York City, The New York Times, Bicycle USA, Essence, Science Probe,* and *The Bicyclist's Sourcebook* (edited by Michael Leccese and Arlene Plevin, Woodbine House, 1991). She is the author of *Bicycling Around New York City: A Gentle Touring Guide* (Menasha Ridge Press, 1994) and is working on books on bicycle commuting and bicycling with children.

She lives with her husband, historian of science Dr. Craig B. Waff, and daughter, Roxana, in Cleveland, Ohio (they previously resided in Maplewood, New Jersey).

Dale Lally is an experienced solo bicycle tourist and group leader. Born and raised in Kansas City, Missouri, he developed an enduring love of cycling while stationed in Berlin, Germany. It wasn't until finishing college and starting his first job at Marquette University in Milwaukee, Wisconsin, that he was able to get back into cycling. Serious cycling had to wait until he moved his family to Louisville, Kentucky, where the weather enabled him to commute by bike year-round to his job at the University of Louisville. He also rode with the Louisville Wheelmen to the tune of about 5,000 miles annually, including at least eight cycling trips to Europe between 1975 and 1990.

In 1990 the year-round commuting came to an abrupt halt when he moved to Canton, New York, which is about as far north as one can get in New York and still be in the United States. In spite of the weather that cuts the cycling season to about six months a year, however, Dale found great backroads and little traffic that makes northern New York a veritable bicycle heaven. Joining the Canton Bicycle Club (CBC), he became such an effective advocate for cycling that the CBC was able to host not one but two major rallies, GEAR 92 and 97, on behalf of the League of American Bicyclists.

Every year for the past several years, he has managed to take at least one major, self-contained bicycle camping tour, culminating in a tour from Fargo, North Dakota, to Canton in July 1998.